- Trump Card Book 11 -
Satan's Vote
- Biden Your Time-

- Trump Card Book Eleven -
Satan's Vote
- Biden Your Time -

Copyright © 2020 -- by W. Lawrence Lipton.

Books may be ordered through booksellers or by contacting:
www.Amazon.com

———————————

Print Title ID: ASIN: B08R6MYNVY
eBook Title ID: ASIN: B08RB23775

Jacked Design & Illustrations © Guebres Studios
Credit Cover Image: Edom Art

ISBN-13: 9798574476673 (sc)
ISBN-10: (ebk)

Printed in the United States of America
CreateSpace date: 12/25/2020

Sat, Oct 31, 2020:
First Lady Melania Trump puts is perfectly!
"Joe Biden says he could do a better job leading this nation. Apparently when you hide in a basement, you feel safe communicating your wishful thinking."

Classic Joe Biden Quotes:
I think the only reason Clarence Thomas is on the court is because he is black.

You cannot go to a 7-Eleven or a Dunkin' Donuts unless you have a slight Indian accent.

When you're appealing to people's fears and anxieties, you can make some gains.

Every single morning since I've been 27 years old, I've got up and someone's handed me a card like the one I have in my pocket with the schedule on it, of all the things I'm gonna do. I don't know what to do if I didn't have that card.
It's easy being vice president - you don't have to do anything.

Make sure of two things. Be careful - microphones are always hot, and understand that in Washington, D.C., a gaffe is when you tell the truth. So, be careful.

I may be Irish, but I'm not stupid.

Don't tell me what you value. Show me your budget and I'll tell you what you value.

CHAPTERS

CHAPTER ONE – Negativity
**"Don't tell me not to live
Just sit and putter
Life's candy and the sun's
A ball of butter
Don't bring around a cloud
To rain on my parade"**

Negativity dominates the new era and is in sharp contrast to the Hippy-era, as seen in the words from the 1964 musical Funny Girl and the lyrics to "*Don't Rain on My Parade.*"

Think of the attacks on Trump: "*Don't tell me not to fly/I've simply got to/If someone takes a spill/It's me and not you…*"

President wanted the nation to soar, and the opposition kept yelling it should crash. Had he been given his head and allowed to function, the House could have proposed improvements to what has proved to be a defective medical care system.

They could also have promoted a replacement for welfare – a basic universal income that exceeds poverty and would then pay for itself through the economic stimulus it would set in place and through the elimination of both the personal deduction on taxes and some forms or levels of unemployment insurance. When you have a UBI, there should be no reason for homelessness.

Three days before the election, Actor Sean Connery (James Bond 007) died. He was an icon of the symbolic genre-defining the Cold War era; with his passing that era officially ended. Though, it falls on us to recognize that remnant of the era remains in "blame Russia" doctrines of the type used to attack Trump while ignoring the real economic threat posed by a China that has returned to its multi-millennia old mercantile pursuits and "spice trade" or "Silk Road" dominance of global commerce.

As I have pointed out in other books when the Obama-Biden team was elected to serve in the nation's 56th & 57th quadrennial cycle, a chapter of history linked to Stonehenge related Hebrew and Chinese calendar structure came to an end. The election of Donald Trump and the "Drain the Swamp" mantra heralded the dawn of a new era in American history – an era where reality trumped politics – driving traditional politicians and their media cohort running into corners where they frailed about while ranting about Trump being responsible for the crimes and lies they had practiced for decades.

There will be those who don't understand the last reference, but they need only search the references to Trump locking children in cages that were documented by photos taken in 2014 of the cages Obama-Biden constructed to store the kids separated from parents or human trafficking coyotes.

Even there, with the use of "coyote", we have comedy – like the October 2020 reaction to Trump's use of the term by actor David Hogg, who believed it to be some form of racist "xenophobia" that was intended to describe the children's parents. But then, Joe Biden had believed that the medically advised practice of sealing the border to those traveling from pandemic infected regions was a form of "racist xenophobia."

The candidacy of Joe Biden introduced a new era – it is the era Trump once alluded to, an era where high public officials could boast of blackmailing foreign governments in a dramatic fact-based manner and openly implicate the President of the United States in Federal {18USC} and foreign {Ukranian} legal violations law.

As the record established, later factual data showed the basis for the blackmail was personal gain via funds laundered through his son's firm. The blackmail involved a Ukrainian criminal who was under investigation, and the goal of the blackmail was to have the investigating prosecutor fired. In any State in the Union, such a confession accompanied by ample documentation would lead to the immediate arrest of the braggart.

Congressman Adam Schiff lied about overwhelming evidence in the Trump impeachment – yet he couldn't identify any statutory to apply it to. With Biden, "overwhelming evidence" includes a public confession that applies to Federal crimes in 18USC, and is now augmented by the documentation from Hunter Biden's laptop. So where are the "overwhelming evidence" claims now?

The blackmail – for personal gain via the millions laundered by Hunter Biden's firm – is also a violation of Ukrainian law and as

Biden was Vice President, that too makes it an impeachable crime.

But, as House Speaker Nancy Pelosi explicitly lied when she stated that "nobody is above the law," it is clear that, for the Swamp Denizens she represents, Joseph Biden is not only above the law, he is exempt from any reasonable application of American laws.

With 50.8% of the popular vote – subject to adjustment due to improper vote counts – and the possibility of 290 Electoral votes, a week after the election it appeared that Biden was President-elect; even if Trump's challenges succeeded, we have a clear affirmation of millions of Americans declaring Biden "above the law."

The people knowingly voted to exempt Biden from any-and-all culpability for the crimes he bragged of committing; they voted to exempt him from any legal action related to the laundered bribe money that was passed through Hunter Biden's firm; they are on record as saying, with their ballots, that it is acceptable to use Air Force 2 as transportation to conduct private business for personal gain.

A slim majority of Americans have spoken. Criminal conduct is not a problem with voters – it's all about personality and, when it comes to Trump, his personality is "not Presidential."

Back in 1992, political strategist James Carville informed Bill Clinton, "It's the economy stupid." But, in 2020, the economy was meaningless; the pandemic dominated in an environment defined by being "Not Trump" – things revolved around the classic political personality trait of "kissing babies" – or, in the case of Joe Biden, sniffing hair and being touchy-feely. If it were still the economy, or if people could see past the media rants about cases of Covid-19, it would mean the voters recognized that Trump had encouraged the record low unemployment, record-high employment for all ethnic groups, and promoted elevated positive numbers for every economic indicator.

Trump's detractors point to slight losses in the agricultural sector. But those losses are part of the restructuring of trade with China and only temporarily affected a half dozen large agribusiness corporations – global warming is having a far greater impact, and even the most aggressive action to combat warming can have no effect until well after 2050.

Some prefer to rant about Trump leaving the Paris Climate Accord, but ignore the fact that the countries that remained in it have met their commitments by exporting their CO2 generation activities to third world nations – none of those nations have made any real change. But under Trump – who was attacked by Biden's Cabal when he suggested creating a solar energy generating fence along the Southern Border – Texas now produces more renewable energy from solar and wind than the coal industry produces energy for the whole nation.

Trump doesn't act through symbolic accords, he encourages business to obey the economic rules which now make solar and wind the only rational energy source for a hi-tech economy.

Where were Pelosi, Schumer, and Biden when China issued its mandate to have only electric cars after 2025? Did they boldly promote America to do the same? Or, is it that they just want the symbolic agreement that requires action after 2030 – when, if they are still alive, Pelosi will be 90, Schumer 79, and Biden 88. It's clear they have a dog in this fight and there is not going to be any rational "Green New Deal" that would grow the economy through the rest of the century and into the next, so it's not the economy.

By 4 November, the election had been reduced to six swing states — Georgia, Michigan, Nevada, North Carolina, Pennsylvania, and Wisconsin. Looking at the Red & Blue election map, many areas were heavily Red, but the major population centers were Blue – and, in those states that had significant Covid-19 outbreaks, the highest fatality areas were predominantly Blue states or Blue districts within Red states.

As of the end of the day, the media was calling 264 Electoral votes for Biden and 214 for Trump. They were doing so, even as the more official count was allowing only the possibility Biden had 253 E.C. votes. And, as of the 10th, Biden had his apparent victory and two states were still in doubt, while one – Georgia – was prepping for a run-off election to determine their Senate representation and possibly which party would take control of the Senate in 2021.

In the meantime, Pelosi refuses to take responsibility for the Democrat's loss of House seats. Before the outcome, Pelosi had told reporters: *"House Democrats are poised to further strengthen our majority—the biggest, most diverse, most dynamic women-led House majority in history."* Afterward, she was spinning things to say she deserves credit for *"winning the majority,"* when the reality is she blew part of Democratic control and her actions are such that I can project a Republican-controlled House in 2023.

The likelihood of things shifting Red is enhanced by Biden's traditional approach to politics – he lies about trivia and significant but meaningless things. Biden's MSM team is attacking Trump for not conceding the election – but, the record shows, Biden lied and is therefore attacking Trump for honoring the commitment Biden made during the first presidential debate when he told Fox News anchor Chris Wallace he would *"pledge not to declare victory until the election is independently certified."*

Biden told Wallace:

"Yes, and here's the deal, we're going to count the ballots as you pointed out, some of these ballots in some states can't even be opened until election day. And if there's thousands of ballots, it's going to take time to do it. Once the winner is declared after all of the ballots are counted, all of the votes are counted, that will be the end of it. That will be the end of it. And if it's me, in fact, fine. If it's not me, I'll support the outcome."

So we know that he was fully committed to withholding his victory claim until after a proper certification of the outcome. But, with the counts still going on, and two states going into a recount, Biden declared victory. And the MSM is castigating Trump because he is waiting for various jurisdiction to confirm their outcome and complete counting the overwhelming number of mail-in ballots.

Having broken his commitment to honoring the process, it didn't take long before China's foreign ministry spokesperson Wang Wenbin says China *"has taken note of Mr. Biden declaring victory, and we understand that the election results will be confirmed according to related U.S. laws and procedures."*

Rather than concede, Trump moved into the normal next phase in the transfer of power – just as he would when handling a finished project or finalized investment – he positioned for his and his family's next stage.

In his business context, he was exploring creating a media outlet; in the political context, he informed his advisors he might be considering a presidential run in 2024 – effectively considering the possibility of becoming the next Grover Cleveland.

Julian Zelizer, a Princeton University professor of political history, noted how Trump's election behavior differed from that of past one-term presidents it that he was not focused on combating opposing party legislators to complete work on legislation or other issues.

Trump allowed Pelosi to block the 2nd stimulus through the addition of tons of costly pork. Since Pelosi's legislative diet is not kosher, there is no reason for Trump to get involved in a problem his successor will need to address and very quickly solve. After all, Biden fails to return the economy to pre-pandemic growth and he dooms Pelosi's House in 2022 and Democratic control of the Oval in 2024. If the pandemic continues, it's on Biden.

Four years of a failed Harris-Biden pair of administrations might well ensure Trump being the next Glover Cleveland – the man who was both the 22nd and 24th POTUS after, as with Trump he was denied a consecutive second term.

Having been implicated in the Ukrainian blackmail, Obama had avoided endorsing Biden. But with the pre-election polling indicating a Biden win, and the fact that post-election – while not the broad support the polls indicated – the results supported Biden as President-elect, Obama chimed in to denounce the Election fraud claims and asserting they were introducing "a dangerous path".

As we know, Obama was also implicated as one of those who initiated the construction of that path with the bogus and irrational claims of Russian interference in the 2016 process to favor Trump. But readers of this series are aware that, if there had been election interference, it would have been in favor of Hillary and focused only on those regions of the nation that had solid wifi coverage.

Still, in a 12 November "60 Minutes" interview, Obama said: *"I'm more troubled by the fact that other Republican officials who clearly know better are going along with this, are humoring him in this fashion. It is one more step in delegitimizing not just the incoming Biden administration, but democracy generally, and that's a dangerous path."*

Millions of dollars in taxpayer funds were wasted efforts to delegitimize Trump and cripple the nation based on lies formulated immediately after the 2016 election. Now we have a nation that, in a single-minded blind effort to remove Trump, has seen fit to install a man who is cognitively impaired and publically bragged of a quid pro quo Ukrainian blackmail violating both American and Ukrainian laws.

What is Obama's complaint? That Trump wants to ensure every legal vote is counted, that the technology used to count those votes is sound and free of technical glitches, that ALL those elected are elected because the majority of legal voters have democratically declared they should be in office?

As Senate Majority Leader Mitch McConnell (R-Ky.) has said, Trump is *"100 percent within his rights [to] weigh his legal options"* in the election. And Trump certainly has the right not to concede an unverified election while votes are still being validated and counted. If nothing else, the financial markets approve.

Whether or not one wishes to accept financial approval, there are transparency issues that must be addressed and are a source of rational concern to any not captivated by the magnificent beauty of "The Emperor's New Clothes."

Not everyone will view the "Emperor's Clothes" in the same way. On 15 November, a New York Times Op-ed asserted: *"No Voter fraud, says the NYT. How stupid are we supposed to be?"*

The piece challenged the NYT lawyer's lie phrasing that there was, "No Evidence of Voter Fraud in Any of the 50 States." It then made pointed out that the statement was *"a bald-faced falsehood. Suspicious ballots...into the millions... are under review in all the contested states...PA, AZ, GA, NV, WI, MI."* The lawyers lie being the assertion that there was no evidence – something that would be true until there was an investigation that would bring the facts together to provide the evidence.

However, it is already known that there was the mysterious Dominion Voting Systems software "vote-flip glitch" that shifted thousands of votes from Trump to Biden at a precise point in time.

As the piece pointed out, *"Some 600,000 votes in Michigan*

that were marked for Trump ended up for Biden. Oh, machine malfunction. Aha. Funny how it never malfunctions in Trump's favor."

As we know, Nancy Pelosi boasted of the use of what she identified as the "wrap-up smear" – a lie that is then repeated in the media, and the fact that it is in the media is then used by the liars to assert its truth – that it has been affirmed or "documented" even though there are no objective facts to support it.

We know the computer "glitch" has been acknowledged, and we also know that there are instances where votes mysteriously and inexplicably moved from Trump to Biden after the reported counts had appeared in the media.

Similar issues appear in the context of Covid-19 and the idea that is as bad as the 1918 Flu Epidemic. And yet, everything we know about it is that it is less deadly than tobacco and only affects those with underlying conditions which would probably have seen them dead six to twelve months later. This is underscored by the 15 November report of findings from the National Cancer Institute (INT) of the Italian city of Milan, in which it was discovered 11.6% of 959 healthy volunteer subjects enrolled in a lung cancer screening trial between September 2019 and March 2020 had coronavirus antibodies well before the first case was identified on 21 February.

Giovanni Apolone, a co-author of the study, told Reuters that *"This is the main finding: people with no symptoms not only were positive after the serological tests but had also antibodies able to kill the virus. It means that the new coronavirus can circulate among the population for long and with a low rate of lethality not because it is disappearing but only to surge again."*

The earliest identified carrier in the study was October 2019 and supports a September infection of a virus that had made its way to Italy before it was formally identified in Wuhan, China. This fact implies it might also have reached New York City before the first identified American case. If so, neither De Blasio nor Trump could be held accountable – even though Mayor Bill De Blasio took actions that encouraged the spread in New York City and its suburbs.

Covid is a culling virus pandemic that has harmed America

and Italy far more than it did its more populous place of origin. But it is not the danger that the weaponized politicization by Pelosi et al infers – and Pelosi's documented actions prove she knows it.

We also have indications of data anomalies and statistical information that might support and aid in identifying instances of some procedural misconduct or election fraud. More importantly, it could reveal the existence of practice runs by hackers or bad actors who intend to manipulate future elections after they release a new and deadly pandemic wave. We need true transparency and levels of objective verification in the election process.

Earlier on the 4th, it was still being projected that Trump had a chance, and the DJIA moved up about 820 points; when the Biden win became apparent, the DJIA gave back 500 points and began to echo a downward trend seen through most of October. But then, as it was clear Biden had probably won – with a loss of some House seats and the probability the Republicans would continue to control the Senate – the DOW set a new record high, and hi-tech firms that had profited from online pandemic shopping leveled off. AOC now wants to tax those event-driven profits.

Election week ended on 6 November, with the DJIA closing down a meaningless 66.78 points; on Saturday, the media declared Biden the winner, making Kamala Harris the first Asian and female Vice President. She was not the first minority Vice President – that honor had fallen on 31st Vice President, Republican Charles Curtis – a Kansas born Native American member of the Kaw Tribal Nation.

By Monday, 9 November, MSM reports announced there was a 90% effective vaccine against Covid-19 and the promise that the economy could return to normal – news that helped drive the DJIA into its new record territory.

There was a concerted MSM effort to avoid mentioning and reminding voters that Trump had promised there would be a vaccine around the time of the election and that it might be available for use before the new year. Of course, Trump had been optimistic and the approval process was such that the release date would be April 2021.

The suggested vaccine release date places Biden in the "Rock-and-hard-place" style situation style that could destroy his legacy and the Democratic Party. The technology involved with the vaccine is a non-traditional genetic engineering related one; there are no real means of testing the long-term effects.

If the vaccine creates any adverse effects, it might not show until after those taking it have children. And if such adverse consequences emerged, anti-vaxxers would be vindicated and Biden's administration would be to blame for a failure to use its three months in office to validate the genetic safety of a vaccine's use in age groups not part of those we know to be subject to the Covid-19 culling effect.

Interestingly, Dr. Ezekiel Emanuel, who was announced as Biden's pick for his Coronavirus Task Force, wrote a 2014 essay that was published in The Atlantic in which explained why he hoped to die at age 75, and why the idea of living past that date to be morally problematic. Thus, Biden's age when he assumes office is beyond the morally problematic point, and life extension for those targeted by Covid-19 {use of ventilators or extreme measures} would also be morally problematic.

As for the virus itself? The U.S. confirmed 10 million cases and 237,860 deaths – representing just over 3% of the population of which 2.3% of the infected died, but that also meant only 0.07% of the total population had been impacted and then only because they were old and/or suffering from life-ending medical conditions.

Even though it was the most populous nation and the one with a level of social mobility and interaction that encourages the spread of the virus, in terms of deaths per million, the United States ranked tenth in the world. And interestingly, Sweden, which had ignored any extreme response or reaction to the pandemic ranked 18th with only 0.06% of its New York City size population dying.

Had Mayor Bill De Blasio acted intelligently if he had taken an approach similar to the Swedish one, New York City might not have suffered nearly 34 thousand deaths – roughly five and a half times the number reached by Sweden. But then, the differences between the Swedish and American numbers might be the product of how and when the numbers are reported. But then, by December the cases and deaths were increasing in Sweden.

In February 2021, we will see how Biden-Harris address the pandemic issue, and learn if their approach builds or destroys the

American economy. In Chapter 6, there is a challenge for Biden to achieve what Trump had shown could be done, and to do it within the first 600-days of his administration.

Satan's Votes were counted and it was a close call. But on the 7th of November, with three states yet to be decided, the media called the election for Biden with 279 Electoral Votes to Trumps 214. Those who want an end to the Electoral College were slapped in the face – if the nation had to await the popular vote, those three states would have been critical. The House and Senate majorities had yet to be determined, and without the Electoral College, there would be no basis for projecting the Biden victory.

Not that it matters, but whether Satan's preferred candidate won-or-lost was something to be discovered after 21 January 2021.

What was important is that there was a shot at arranging the succession in a manner that places POTUS-49 in office in 2033.

As those who have read my Hebrew Calendar and prophecy interpretation books know, 49 is an ancient unit of measure called the OMER. Many of us are familiar with the Aladdin story in which we are told of importance derived from being the seventh son of a seventh son – that is, the 49th in succession within a period of just three generations. Historically, mystical powers are associated with astronomy derived from the ancient calendar system.

The number 49 can be viewed as akin to units such as a dozen or a baker's dozen – comically, these are akin to the Twelve Tribes of Israel plus a 13th group that constituted the ruling Levite and Kohanim. Because the Levites claimed "no inheritance" it can be seen as "comical" because, by inheritance, they ruled all of Israel, and when they were evicted "Ten Tribes' were said to be lost, yet all survived and prospered under a different north-south structure.

The ancestral lines of American Presidents and most of those recognized as famous are part of the same line of descent that was to yield the Crown Princes of Europe and the principal leaders in America – including its most famous movie stars, who were and are either descendant from the 4-Sisters or Jewish.

To understand this, consider "black" actress Meghan Markle who married Prince Harry, became the 'Duchess of Sussex' and is routinely referred to as being 'Black'. The media ignores the fact her ancestry is also Jewish and that, among others, she and Harry share the 3rd Baron De Hungerford as their 15th great-grandfather.

Kamala Harris is a non-POTUS Cousin who is married to a Jewish man and became the 49th Vice President – the first female to occupy that office – indicating the significance of 49 in the 2020 election. But, she's not family and cannot become POTUS.

There is comedy reflected in America as the original colonies and the ruling elite are POTUS Cousins who were also descendants of the 4-Sisters who descended from Charlemagne the Great.

As with all creatures, there is always a ruling elite, the Queen Bee whose direct descendants rule the hive and whose death can bring an end to the hive. There is also the Lead Stallion or Lion King whose domination of the herd or pride is also genetic, but can be seen in a more mobile society.

Where Trump was a stallion turning a stampeding herd, will Harris become the Queen Bee whose role determines the death and life of the Hive?

And what of Biden? Why was he fated to win? Was he just finally in the right place, at the right time, with the right credentials?

You'll have the answers in Chapter 5. But, for now… there is a bit of groundwork to lay.

When Rome ended the Levite rule over Israel and scattered the Hebrews, the Hebrews reverted from a Hive to Herd culture. If the leadership of America ceases to have the Hive structure, it will, like Spain and France, fall from its global leadership role.

In a speech that promised to unify the nation, Biden accepted the preliminary election results and his destiny by saying: *"Let us be the nation that we know we can be. A nation united, a nation strengthened, a nation healed."*

At the time of his speech, it appears that 75 million people voted for him, and 71 million for Trump. Though the Social Media was discussing the irregularities which were coming to light – there were hundreds of thousands of ballots found in trash bins or that simply appeared; in one instance there was the claim of over 100 thousand ballots being delivered which were all for Biden and none

for Trump; in some cases, ballots had no votes for local issues –
and that infers the individuals intentionally avoided or expressed
no interest in, local issues or House and Senate elections.

Trump representatives let it be known they would launch
legal challenges in various states and districts, but it is unlikely that
this will change the outcome – though it could undermine popular
confidence in the election process in an era when it was the Pelosi-
Schumer Democrats who asserted American elections were being
rigged or interfered with by foreign actors. Yet they rebelled when
Trump made a similar assertion about Biden's victory.

Biden has promised to undo the Trump tax policies and that
means those who have made a profit since the March 2020 bottom
will need to sell in 2020 or lose their profits to the combination of
the Biden confiscatory tax plan and an incompetent fiscal policy
that promises to shift all economic power and control to China.

Any credible proof of election ballot tampering might serve
to shift attention away from the Pelosi-Schumer Cold War-era style
attacks on Russia and China – augmented by evidence the Biden
family are long-time establish Manchurian Candidates.

The combined total for Pennsylvania (20), North Carolina
(15), and Georgia (16) were offered Trump a possibility of receiving
51 Electoral votes which would bring him to 265 – five short of the
270 needed for re-election. But, the possibility that the Fake News
media had biased their projections without proper regard for the
record number of uncounted absentee, mail-in, or early votes was
still in play. That ended on Friday the Thirteenth when tabulations
were reported and CNN showed Biden winning 306 Electoral Votes
to Trump's 232.

But given that, by the time Biden gave his acceptance
speech, the Electoral College Alexandria Ocasio-Cortez {AOC} and
others had so strongly denounced when it gave the 2016 victory to
Trump were now seeing it give Biden a commanding 290 votes
when only 270 were needed, and a possibility of achieving 321.

This raises yet another "but" to be considered: Richard M.
Nixon received 96.65% percent of the Electoral votes and carried 49
states with 60.7% of the popular vote – he proved to be a crook who
resigned from office to avoid impeachment and prosecution.

Unfortunately, as we have seen throughout this book series – and as predicted in my March 2014 book, *'Death Over Life: Secret of Revelation: A Prophecy of America's Destruction'* – America has entered a phase where it is determined to self-destruct, and in doing so, fulfill ancient prophecies. Thus, it makes sense the nation would want a President who openly and freely confessed to illegally blackmailing a foreign government for what we now know was the personal financial benefit of himself and his family.

In many ways, European based societies have triggered what might be called a societal "reset." We will soon see India and China reemerge – and China prevail – to be the controlling cultures in an otherwise backward world. Certainly, this election set the stage for an incompetent female of Indian origin to take command of the Oval Office while China commands modern merchant trade in the same way it controlled the spice trade in the days of the Silk Road.

With his victory, and affirmation of Pelosi Swamp Denizens retaining their slim control of the House of Representatives, Biden remains above the law and his family might become exempt from punishment for all aspects of their proven corruption.

While a Red Wave could take control of the House in 2022, it will be too late. Biden's mental detrition will become so pervasive as to require his removal, for medical reasons, under Article 25; it would then fall on Kamala Harris to issue a Presidential Pardon for any-and-all crimes that can be linked to Biden and, therefore, to his family. Joseph R. Biden becomes Richard M. Nixon 2.0.

The election results both affirm a POTUS Cousin can defeat a non-Cousin and reveal that roughly half the nation decided it would prefer a self-confessed criminal over a sitting POTUS who has simply been accused of wrongdoing – albeit with claims that there is "overwhelming evidence" of crimes they cannot define or in any way cite.

Had they been able to cite a crime, it would have been cited as part of the Articles of Impeachment and Trump would have been removed from office and Mike Pence would have been POTUS, the historic connection to the 4-Sisters would have been broken, and the Great Experiment would have come to an end.

Instead, in 2020, the nation voted in record numbers and a

close race decided to give Joe Biden his last hurrah, and possibly allow him to become the 8th president to die in office.

Should Biden be removed due to cognitive deterioration, or because he falls victim to the zero-year curse that has seen five of the eight Presidents first elected in a year ending in zero die, the nation will have its first female President and see the 4-Sisters connection broken by someone with no connection to POTUS Cousins.

As covered in my 2017 book, *Jonathon's POTUS Cousins*, if we look at election tradition, Van Buren, Trump, and Jefferson were not POTUS Cousins; In the cases of Trump and Jefferson, their Cousin connection was by marriage. However, both men were descendants of the 4-Sisters and thus gained validity to hold the office. When Hillary ran, she too was only connected by marriage, but without the genetic ancestry dating back to the sisters in 1170 and through them to Emperor Charlemagne.

With Van Buren, the issue is a lack of ancestral information prior to the mid-sixteenth century. The best we can do is assume he could have been part of the ancient ancestral leadership lineage.

Granted, some reject the idea of herd leadership or ancestral importance. However, they will still speak of Trump as not being "Presidential" or someone being of the "wrong" social class or – as in the case of Kamala – societal caste.

Using Kamal as an example, while she is not from the proper European ancestral line of nobility – though she have some British nobility in her ancestry – her mother is from India and gave her the middle name "Devi", meaning *"supreme goddess, often identified with Parvati and Shakti."* Parvati associates her with the mother of two Hindu deities and might well be keyed back to my 2011 book, *"Grandpa Was A Deity: How A Tribal Assertion Created Modern Culture."*

Kamala's mother, Gopalan Shyamala, was a biochemist and, therefore, we can assume a higher level of intelligence that would normally be associated with the Brahmin Caste which is related to the Hebrew Ashkenazi Levites.

In 2003, Gopalan Shyamala stated, *"In Indian society, we go by birth. We are Brahmins, that is the top caste. Please do not confuse this with class, which is only about money. For Brahmins, the bloodline is the most important."*

Based on her Caste, Kamala does belong to an ancient line of national leaders and affirmed that lineage connection through her 2004 marriage to an Ashkenazi Jew – who, in January 2021, will become both the first *"second gentlemen"* and first Jewish Vice Presidential spouse in American history.

America is in an era of change and social growth.

Trump initiated one level of change through Ivanka. After the Clintons left office, their daughter married a Jewish man but she retained her religious ties. Ivanka married an Orthodox Jewish man and converted – presenting America with an Orthodox Jewish "First Daughter" for the first time in history.

Now, by shattering the glass ceiling, Kamala introduced a new level of firsts which compliments the traditional ties to the 4-Sisters and lessens the disruptive potential that had defined similar transitions in Europe.

Anti-Semites and racists might be shaken by a dual prospect presented by the Harris-Emhoff duo, but those who are locked into the Bible predictions for this will recognize the emergence of an event that could be seen as fulfillment and affirmation of their beliefs.

If it were to turn out that Douglas Emhoff belonged to a DNA haplotype group designated R1a or was a Kohanim J2 carrying the Cohen Modal Haplotype, the historical linkage would be perfect and completely negate the need for the Charlemagne connection.

On her other side, Kamala's father, Dr. Donald Jasper Harris, is an economist and professor emeritus at Stanford University. So, once again, we have indications of high intelligence and a leadership ancestry worthy of the Oval Office.

Her father is Jamaican by birth, and that would mean there is a level of interbred African and British ancestry which goes way beyond the stated connection to the noted Irish-born Jamaican slave owner Hamilton Brown.

Unfortunately, as with Van Buren, we lack the genealogical data to link Kamala's Hamilton Brown ancestry to the others of that name who are established to be descendants of the 4-Sisters. Were such a documented connection, Kamala would belong to a family line that transcends American, European, and Asian leaders.

As a nation, America is free to eke out all the negativity it can handle. MSM has already reported on the rioters or protesters who are totally down on the nation but still remain here – because, for all the imagined and occasionally real faults, America is still the greatest nation in history.

But this is a transitional point in history and we can expect a wide range of discord and disturbance. In a series based on 57, Trump's election was the 58th, or first in the new historic phase.

Biden was destined to win – be it the historic Cousins pattern or destiny – maybe even Satan's Vote was in play. But would Satan want Biden or Trump? Or does he just want their non-Cousin vice president to take the reins?

Had the Impeachment worked, Pence would be POTUS and the first outside to hold that office which was not of the traditional line. He gets another shot with Harris.

	Deaths:	Population:	%	Median
2009	2,437,163	306,771,529	0.79%	Age
2010	2,468,435	309,346,863	0.80%	37.2
2011	2,515,458	311,718,857	0.81%	37.3
2012	2,543,279	314,102,623	0.81%	37.4
2013	2,596,993	316,427,395	0.82%	37.6
2014	2,626,418	318,907,401	0.82%	37.7
2015	2,712,630	321,418,820	0.84%	37.8
2016	2,744,248	323,071,342	0.85%	37.9
2017	2,813,503	325,147,121	0.87%	38.0
2018	2,839,205	327,167,439	0.87%	38.2
2019	2,330,395	328,239,523	0.71%	38.4
2020		331,558,077		38.3
Average (2009-2018)			0.83%	
2019	2,717,775	Anticipated		
	387,380	Shortfall		
2020	2,745,252	Anticipated		
		Covid-19		

Then there is Covid-19. The culling virus has inflicted more change, with less death' than any pandemic in history. Could that be how Satan cast his ballot? Shall we see {in 2021}?

With Coronavirus a focus of widespread attention, and given that I have repeatedly asserted it to be a "culling virus", it seemed appropriate to provide a historic perspective for deaths in America. The chart shows deaths, the population, and the percentage of that population that died in the period of the Obama and Trump Administrations from 2009 to 2019.

To the right of those numbers, we have the median population age in each year. Below the numbers, we see a 10-year average of the death percentages. And below that, the calculated deaths based on that average as applied to the 2019 population.

As we can see, 387,380 FEWER people died than adhering to a 10-year average would require.

Apply the same average to the 2020 population, or simply say those who did not die in 2019 would in 2020, and we can anticipate that the total 2020 death rate would reach – WITHOUT the Covid-19 – on average, 2,745,252.

Unless that number is exceeded significantly, Covid-19 has made no actual difference in American mortality rates. But it might provide future benefits.

The reason for the "significantly" is basic demographics. The population of those nations which were active participants in World War Two experienced the Baby-Boom. As many know, after a war or extensive natural catastrophe, populations compensate for the loss of life by having a population explosion.

After wars, the bias is toward sons outnumbering daughters – it appears there is a male-stress-related component associated with fertility-gender. Normally, the bias favors the conception and birth of 105 males for every 100 females. With Covid-19, we see the ratio holds (approximately) and we are seeing more elderly males die than elderly females.

In a perverse way, the natural Baby-Boom distortion in the ratio is being repeated. Could it be that this is "Satan's Vote" – the way the mythical Satan carries out the will of his divine boss?

The Right-wing Conservatives are noted for waving Bibles – and the Book of Revelation proclaims there shall be, in the second millennium, death of a third of all life.

We are in a perverse period – one where the numbers 56 and 57 seem to be, as we shall see in subsequent chapters, in play. But, at this point, and before we play with the way Covid-19, Climate Change, and Obama vs Trumpism seem to be coming together on schedule, there a curious coincidence about the founding of the nation and aspects of the Bible.

After we've looked at the events marking the end of the Trump era as POTUS, we will play with the strange similarities. For now, it is sufficient to say, the nation was founded on the signatures of the 56-men who signed the Declaration of Independence.

CHAPTER TWO – Ready to Fail
"Az ikh vel zayn vi yener,
"If I am to be like someone else,
ver vet zayn vi ikh?"
who will be like me?"

Well, here we are in the 2nd chapter of Book-11 of the Trump Card series. In Book-10 we continued to point out that Covid-19 was a Culling Virus and the apparent fact that, without the virus, those who died would have done so within six months to a year was being ignored by the media – instead MSM focused on the 95-percent of cases which proved to be asymptomatic.

There are common elements that define Covid-19 fatalities – pre-existing potentially fatal medical conditions or being a male who has exceeded the current average human life expectancy of 73.2 years (75.6 years for females and 70.8 years for males).

An examination of Covid-19 statistics reveals the outbreak had initially focused on first-world nations that were highly mobile and socially interactive. The restrictive nature of Chinese society served to control the spread there, while the highly mobile and interactive culture of the United States spawned the highest per capita number of cases of any nation.

Naturally, while the spread was most severe in Democratic strongholds, the vocal swamp denizens within the Democratic Party made it a point to yell about Trump mishandling things – when, if he had done what they had initially promoted, things would have been far worse. As a result, there was a health-related propaganda bias against Trump added to 46-months of baseless impeachment spawning propaganda.

But this was not unanticipated, rather it was necessary or the prediction/prophecy of my 2014 book, "Death Over Life," could not be fulfilled.

In that book, using the Birther assertions as a focal point, I pointed to the cognitive dissonance or irrationality that had come to dominate swamp controlled thinking:

"Barack Obama was born in Honolulu, two years after

*Hawaiian statehood – making him a 'natural born America';
Rafael Edward 'Ted' Cruz was born in Calgary, Alberta,
Canada – rending him a 'natural born Canadian'. Those
called Birthers attack Obama as ineligible to hold the Office of
President, but find no inconsistency in supporting a Cruz
candidacy for the office in 2016.*

We have seen the same logical inconsistency with the
assertion of an improper *"quid pro quo"* when Trump invoked the
1998 Clinton Treaty and asked Ukraine to provide the Attorney
General with any Burisma or other investigation data involving the
Biden family; yet there was no outrage when, in 2018, Joe boasted
of his *"quid pro quo"* blackmailing of the Ukrainian President into
firing a Prosecutor General investing Burisma – and, by extension,
the millions of dollars being paid to Hunter Biden for access to, and
support from, the Office of the Vice President and by extension the
U.S. State Department.

Imagine what the State Department would say if President
Biden were blackmailed by China – maybe into firing the head of
the CIA or Federal Trade Commission. After all, what is good for a
goose should be good for a gander.

In *Death Over Life*, and in the context of a recession, it was
pointed out they follow a pattern: *"we can expect one in the second
term of whoever is elected in 2016."* Now we know the cycle was
accelerated by the pandemic and will present as the first-term of
the Biden-Harris administration.

But there was also the projection that Congress would play
a medical-related recession triggering game: *"Congress will then
play budgetary games to hamper Obamacare and the nation in
2016 – the result will be a 2017 recession which will make a
mockery of the one in 2007."*

Those games were impeded by the Impeachment and
weren't begun until February 2020, when the pandemic created a
necessity to revamp the process under the guise of being a
"stimulus package" or a means of effective economic compensation.

Covid-19 provided the catalyst for the predicted recession
and established the basis to fulfill both recession predictions, with
the *"Harris-Biden Administration"* screwing up enough to cause
the downturn to morph into an all-out Depression before 2024.

Hillary Clinton was predicted to be the 2016 candidate, the Republican choice was unknown. All that could be said was who would not be a viable candidate; the emergence of Donald Trump had the effect of tilting the perceived trend and gave us this Trump Card book series – the tenth book in the series was, *POTUS FORTY 5.4.2 or 6.4.1: "The Pandemic President"*.

Book-10 was published on 25 September, four days later, on 29 September the world witnessed a debacle identified as the first Presidential Debate, where President Trump had to confront both his opponent and the moderator – both of who were in complete denial of his long record of denouncing White Supremacist groups and bigotry in general. Adding to the nonsense was Biden's long history of racism and promoting laws designed to target minorities.

On 17 September 2008, a New York Times article dealt with Biden's history on the issues of race and female equality – it opened with a Biden quote claiming, *"I wasn't at the bridge at Selma, but the struggle for civil rights was the animating political element of my life."*

The article stated: *"He has been instrumental in expanding voting rights, supporting affirmative action, passing the Violence Against Women Act, expanding the definition of hate crimes, and working toward ending employment discrimination."*

In 1978, Biden had taken a position on school busing that managed to alienate both white and black communities. In 1987, as Chairman of the Senate Judiciary Committee, be opposed the nomination of Conservative Judge Robert Heron Bork whose Constitutional views were too restrictive in the areas of both civil rights and women's rights.

In 1991, Biden oversaw the nomination of Clarence Thomas to the SCOTUS bench – he then omitted mention of Thomas from his 365-page autobiography – thereby avoiding reigniting what he would later term an *"incendiary bomb"* fueled by the issues of race, sex, and affirmative action.

After the nomination was affirmed, Thomas – who made history as only the second African-American to be nominated for the SCOTUS bench – would write an autobiography in which he would accuse Biden of leading a *"high-tech lynch mob."*

As the article reported, later, Senator John C. Danforth of Missouri, a supporter of Thomas, would say, *"I don't go as far as Clarence. I don't think he was the leader of the lynch mob. I think what he was ... was the park superintendent at the site at which the lynching took place."*

That *"park superintendent"* role seems to be the one Biden is best suited for and readily assumes. So much so, the potential Biden-Harris administration would be described by Biden, and his running mate Kamala Harris, as the HARRIS-Biden administration.

The *"park superintendent"* title sounds good, but the reality is that they are college graduates who make less than $20 per hour in an era where the minimum wage in Washington, D.C. is $15. If that *"park superintendent"* was married with one or more children, they qualify for Public Assistance (welfare).

Biden's skill level equates to that of a full-time worker and welfare recipient – a Welfare Queen who lies about their income – and we see the bribes funneled through or laundered by Hunter Biden and the rest of the Biden family as his work, and his salary as an elected official as the welfare contribution.

While Biden hid in his basement, Trump was out doing the work of a President. As a result, on 2 October Trump announced: *"Tonight, FLOTUS and I tested positive for COVID-19. We will begin our quarantine and recovery process immediately. We will get through this TOGETHER!"*

We hear people yell about being "Presidential," but nobody provides a definition or clear example of what that means – other than playing politics without helping the citizens.

Being "Presidential" follows the rules of a servant and not a leader. An intelligent observer would prefer that every president be their own person and not bend to the political establishment. There is no standard for behavior, the President is the Chief Executive and should behave like one – especially since they are overseeing the most powerful economy, and military in the world.

A President should not, as Bush did, lie about who was guilty of an attack on American soil – just so he could justify murdering that individual and initiating a 19-year budget-busting killing spree.

A President should not, as Nixon did, support a break-in and criminal activities against the opposition political party. But, there is a claim to evidence Obama-Biden engaged in a variation on that criminality utilizing the FBI. It was compounded by evidence of Hillary Clinton engaging a Russian agent to create the false Steele Dossier – collusion with a foreign power to interfere or distort an American election.

"If you are to be like someone else, who are you?" And, more importantly, is that someone else the person you want to be?

One thing about Trump, as a PT Barnum type showman, he has perfected the art of the Golden Rule – do to others as they do unto you, and when selling to others, phrase the sale in terms you know they have used in the past.

Election Some 600,000 votes in Michigan that were marked for Trump ended up for Biden. Oh, machine malfunction. Aha. Funny how it never malfunctions in Trump's favor. and improprieties are classic Schumer Swamp Denizen claims. And now that Biden has selected Ronald Klain as White House chief of staff, Klain's 2014 tweet takes on comical significance. It had been posted that, "*68% of Americans think elections are rigged.*" And Klain replied, "*That's because they are.*"

Later he elaborated by asserting: "*Americans think elections are rigged in favor of incumbents. And they're basically right.*" And explained: "*Incumbents get a voice in gerrymandering — meaning that the politicians, in an inversion of the normal rules of democracy, get to choose their voters.*"

Klain took matters a step further by asserting what is a variation on why Trump consistently turns to the courts – even when it is almost a given that he will lose. Klain indicated that "*The term 'rigged' might go a tad far. The problem here isn't fraud. In elections, like in so much else, the scandal is what's legal.*" Thus, the issue becomes one of having the court determine the proper context and phrasing for that which is deemed "legal."

In 2016, the California-NYC Democratic cabal had asserted that Russia rigged the election for Trump. But we now know that the only people working with the Russians were those working for

Hillary Clinton. Still, yelling *"Russia, Russia, Russia"* is little more than a dog-whistle approach to invoking the *"Red Menace"* rhetoric of the McCarthy era when the Baby-Boomers were raised.

They are invoking the same coded or suggestive language that is associated with yelling "socialist" or "socialism" whenever common sense ways to address common problems are suggested to be best handled through the government. In many circumstances, to yell socialist is to declare you are anti-Bible – in both old or new testament form. Medicare For All (M4A) is the Good Samaritan as ruler of the land and someone revered by Jesus – which means any Christian who attacks it is behaving as an anti-Christ.

If you were to Google crooked politicians, you find quotes like this: *"Money and corruption are ruining the land, crooked politicians betray the working man, pocketing the profits and treating us like sheep, and we're tired of hearing promises that we know they'll never keep."* ~Ray Davies

Or, given that Biden is the Manchurian Candidate for 2020, the Italian Mafia has become oriental but this Steve Allen version still applies: *"Ours is a government of checks and balances. The Mafia and crooked businessmen make out checks, and the politicians and other compromised officials improve their bank balances."*

In the 1930s, anarchist political activist and writer Emma Goldman asserted: *"If voting changed anything, they'd make it illegal."* And, when Donald Trump came in with a promise to drain the swamp, it gave rise to the title of the third book in this series *"The Swamp Fights Back"*.

In fighting back, we saw the baseless impeachment and the 2020 record voter turnout that gave Biden the most votes received by any President-elect, and Trump the most votes for a Republican.

We affirmed the idea of a politician as a systemic liar and the exact person the voters want as their leader.

While Trump was called a liar, Biden and his colleagues proved they are liars.

Given the proof, the voters selected the true liar. But, as you know, my bias is that Biden was the winner because he, and not Trump, was the POTUS Cousin in the election – and the POTUS

Cousin always wins. When neither is a POTUS Cousin, as in 2016, the one who is a descendant of the 4-Sisters will be the winner.

During the 29 September 2020 Debate, the world witnessed a persistent demand that Trump repeat what he had consistently stated – that he opposed and condemned White Supremacists.

He was treated as if he had never condemned them, even when he again did so in response to the question. Yet, Biden had stood and praised White Supremacists, had honored leaders of the KKK and other groups – he even proudly received an award named for a racist. Yet, he was not asked to denounce them.

During that questioning, Trump clearly stated, "*I've said it many times, and let me be clear again: I condemn the [Ku Klux Klan]. I condemn all white supremacists. I condemn the Proud Boys. I don't know much about the Proud Boys, almost nothing. But I condemn that.*"

It is funny that Biden-Wallace should have raised the issue of the "Proud Boy" – a group that has Black leaders and exists in Israel as a group that is opposed to things Americans associate with the KKK and other supremacist groups. At the same time, in America and Canada, it is an all-male far-right, neo-fascist, political group that balances the far-left, anti-Antifa, socialists.

That Chris Wallace should push the point in 2020 shows that he is incompetent and not a credible reporter. In 2016, Wallace had posed the same question to Trump and had gotten the response: "*I totally disavow the Ku Klux Klan, I totally disavow David Duke. I've been doing it for two weeks; you're probably the 18th person that's asked me the question.*"

Is it "Presidential" to hold views that are consistent in their opposition to bigotry? Would it be "Presidential" to have decades of behavior that demonstrates that opposition – such as desecrating and reversing the anti-Semitism at Mar-a-Largo immediately upon taking title to that Florida Golf Course?

We can look at those accusing Trump of not being the person Trump has shown himself to be.

Biden promotes laws that attack and imprison Blacks. He has been consistent in his lies – going back to plagiarism he committed in college and continued to engage into the point where it cost him an earlier run for the Oval Office. He stood on the Debate stage and lied about both his past statements and Trump's positions.

To be a liar is being "Presidential", or Biden would not have been the favorite going into the November election.

We can look at those who back Biden – the representatives of California and New York State who encouraged the spreading of the Covid-19 pandemic and had sought to impeach Trump as soon as the 2016 results were announced.

They then lied and blamed Trump for their actions and they also ignored the blatant bragging by Biden of his violation of 18USC laws and the possible criminal activities of his son Hunter Biden relative to receiving $3.5 million from a Russian oligarch, $1.6 Billion from China, and, of course, the millions received from the criminal owner of Ukraine's Burisma.

California is interesting because it sponsors the open borders that would allow it to gerrymander an increase in representatives without any increase in voters. California also tried to pass a law that made ethnic studies a requirement for graduation from high school – an ethnic studies curriculum that denied the Holocaust and, as pointed out by the California Legislative Jewish Caucus had "effectively erases the American Jewish experience," "denigrates Jews," "omits anti-Semitism," and made it a point to "single Israel out for condemnation."

In New York, the pandemic capital of the nation, it wasn't until the night of 5 October 2020 – after President Trump returned to the White House after being treated for Coovid-19 – that New York's Governor Cuomo decided it was time to take action against the spread and signed an order requiring all visitors to New York State to enter a two-week period of isolation upon their arrival.

Had he done that when Trump first issued the Travel Ban, it is likely there would be far fewer cases and many fewer deaths. But at the time Cuomo was too busy placing infected individuals in nursing homes where they could quickly spread the Culling Virus among its target demographic – and from there, across the nation.

Cuomo also singled out the Jewish community for a specific warning aimed at disrupting Religious celebrations and practices.

It is worth noting that, throughout the ages, history makes it clear that religious Jews escaped the most severe effects of the worst pandemics or plagues. This demonstrable fact is derived from their traditional hygienic practices which have since been adopted by the medical profession.

Two weeks after the election, New York City and New Jersey were again going into Thanksgiving Day celebration variation on a lockdown, and several states were seeing virus surges that required a mask mandate.

In the meantime, Biden was playing politics with the failure of states to certify the election – an act that would allow Trump to concede and begin the transition process. However, Trump does not concede if there is a larger legal or strategic benefit.

Biden had already begun to blame Trump for his team's lack of a distribution plan for the various Covid-19 vaccines which were being announced as being available when his administration takes office.

Biden and his staff were making claims that Trump's people were refusing to cooperate with the transition team and, therefore, *"more people may die."* But we would soon learn that there was a vaccine ready and it would be distributed a month before Biden was scheduled to assume office.

But rational citizens realize that the transition has nothing to do with the fact 2% of those who contract the virus will die, and the vaccine could not possibly be administered fast enough to have the preventative effect before February – Biden's team will need to deal with the distribution process that will be initiated during the summer of 2021.

Curiously, even Biden had stated, the vaccine is *"of little use until you're vaccinated. So how do we get the vaccine, how do we get over 300 million Americans vaccinated? What's the game plan?"*

But Biden has no plan for distribution, so he is preparing to blame Trump for the Biden administration's first significant failure.

***CHAPTER THREE** – Problems*
"But now, let's give each other a chance.
It's time to put away the harsh rhetoric.
To lower the temperature.
To see each other again.
To listen to each other again.
~ Biden 2020 Acceptance Speech

In 1963, the voting age was still 21 and two years before I was eligible to vote, Malcolm X gave a speech, a portion of which has become popular because it resonates in the 2020 era of BLM and the anti-Trump:

"The white liberal differs from the white conservative only in one way: the liberal is more deceitful than the conservative. The liberal is more hypocritical than the conservative. Both want power, but the white liberal is the one who has perfected the art of posing as the Negro's friend and benefactor; and by winning the friendship, allegiance, and support of the Negro, the white liberal is able to use the Negro as a pawn or tool in this political "football game" that is constantly raging between the white liberals and white conservatives."

It is curious – 1963 was the period in which John Fitzgerald Kennedy (JFK) was emerging and being a Democrat seemed like the proper role to take.

On 10 June 1963, JFK delivered the commencement address at American University in Washington, D.C. which was to become known as "*A Strategy of Peace*" that outlined a plan to curb nuclear arms – five months later, on 22 November 1963, he would be dead; 15-months after that, on 21 February 1965, Malcolm Little, known as Malcolm X, would also be dead. Both men were assassinated.

In between the assassinations, the Second Indonesian War – more commonly called the Vietnam War – had escalated from the action begun by Eisenhower in 1955. That fit of killing lasted from 1 November 1955 to 30 April 1975 (19 years, 5 months, 4 weeks, and 1 day) and is now rivaled by the Middle eastern conflict begun by George H. W. Bush and expanded upon by his son, George W.

Bush.

Both sets of wars show how devoted to killing America really is.

Ronald Reagan gave us Iran-Contra and the criminal act of trading of arms to Iran as a way of arranging for the release of the American hostages being held in Lebanon.

In terms of the Trump era, Reagan had engaged in a classic *Quid Pro Quo* that looked good politically and actually rewarded the Iranian government responsible for taking Fifty-two American diplomats and citizens hostage during the Carter administration and holding them 444 days {4 November 1979 – 20 January 1981}. Readers might realize, the release coincided with the Inauguration of Reagan – who had, "coincidentally," announced his candidacy on 13 November 1979.

Were the hostages part of political collusion or *quid pro quo* between Reagan and Ayatollah Khomeini to cripple Carter's chance for reelection? Why else would they be released on the day Reagan was inaugurated?

America seems to have a history of racism, violence, and mass destruction keyed to "backdoor deals" for personal political or economic gain.

When it can not be achieved through the killings on foreign soils, groups like BLM achieve their goals via domestic actions that echo the Kristallnacht destruction of minority businesses.

In the 1960s era of Malcolm X and JFK, "race riots" saw the destruction of black communities. In 2020 BLM sponsored similar activities that destroyed Minneapolis businesses owned by Blacks, Latinos, and Muslims. Similar destruction occurred in numerous districts that shared a common element – they were represented by House Managers promoting Trump's impeachment for obedience to Treaty and Law.

Specifically, Trump's requesting – in accordance with a 1998 Clinton-era Treaty – any investigation data, mentioning the Bidens, that Ukraine investigators discover in the prosecution of Burisma and related companies engaged in criminal activities. Per the terms of the Treaty, that data was to be passed to the Attorney General.

Keep in mind that Biden had very publically bragged about

his, Obama approved *quid pro quo* blackmail of Ukraine so they would fire Prosecutor General Shokin, which could have brought an end to the Burisma investigation and protected Hunter Biden.

In 2019, after the nation witnessed President Trump raising the earnings of minorities, lowered their unemployment rate, and raised their rate of full-time gainful employment, BLM emerged to destroy all that had been gained. Then, along came Covid-19, and individuals like New York City Mayor Bill De Blasio joined with BLM demonstrators to attack the President and inflict greater harm to the minority neighborhoods under his jurisdiction.

For De Blasio it was easy, he simply made decisions that ensured New York City would become the pandemic death capital of the nation – so long as most of those deaths were in Black or Latino neighborhoods. He even tossed in a bit of anti-Semitism by tailoring his restrictions to harm the religious freedom of Orthodox Jews.

As Malcolm X had stated, "*the liberal is more deceitful than the conservative.*" More specifically, the Swamp denizens who had behind the liberal Democratic label are the deceivers of men who are at the core of destruction and harm to both the nation and global community.

As we know, Biden has shown himself to be "Above the Law" when it comes to graft and the blackmailing of foreign nations for personal or family gain. It has yet to be established how deceitful Kamala Harris is. However, she was a prosecutor and therefore is skilled in "Lawyer's Lies", which are the highest form of deceit.

In August 2020, it was revealed that, in 2008, when she was a D.A., Harris prosecuted an innocent man for murder, despite the fact there was nothing to tie him to the crime besides the fact that the victim had been his friend. Jamal Trulove was sentenced to death based on the false testimony of one witness who contracted the evidence and excluded testimony of witnesses who substantiated the exculpatory evidence.

Eventually, Trulove's lawyer was able to reverse the verdict and Trulove was awarded a $13 million settlement based on witness manipulation, fabrication of evidence, and police misconduct that had led to his wrongful conviction.

In a case involving a man named Kevin Cooper, who was accused of killing two adults and two children, Harris ignored the exculpatory evidence which would have exonerated Cooper – thus she effectively allowed the real killer to escape justice while sending an innocent man to death row. Harris was lambasted by Candidate Tulsi Gabbard for this and other acts that sent innocent black men to prison.

In other cases, verdicts won by Harris were reversed based on defense attorney malfeasance which should have been caught by the prosecutor; in the case of Daniel Larsen, even after it was shown that he was innocent, Harris blocked his release from prison for two years. Her reason for ignoring the exculpatory evidence, including testimony from a police officer who placed Larsen 35 miles away at the time of the crime, was a paperwork filing deadline technicality.

For Harris, filing paperwork on an arbitrarily set schedule is superceded irrefutable evidence of innocence. This creates some interesting possibilities for a person with that mindset who might well apply it to using nuclear launch codes against North Korea, Iran, or even China and Russia.

However, the Harris-Biden camp supporters have played or introduced an interesting scenario – what if Trump refuses to leave office?

It's a question revealing exactly how dim-witted they believe their followers to be. They asserted that Trump not only doesn't wish to move out of the White House, he would violate the law and stay.

The ignorant assertion infers they believe Trump believes he could still legislation into law and command the military. The idiots would have their dim-witted follower to believe a man raised in the real estate industry, a rental property developer, believes he can stay in residence after his lease expires.

Who in government would give their support to the one-man "coup" that these demented individuals were promoting?

It's *"The Emperor's New Clothes"* – where the garments in question are the idea that a man who always utilizes the law would violate that law; that a man who is concerned with his place in the history books would place himself among the demented crazies who are comic footnotes.

The scenario was accompanied by the idea that he would not concede the election while votes were still being counted and before any states had certified their results.

On Thanksgiving, a direct question on whether he would leave office allowed Trump to make his position clear.

Specifically, when asked, "*If the Electoral College does elect President-elect Biden, are you not going to leave the building?*" Trump responded, "*Just so you know...certainly, I will, certainly I will. And you know that, but I think that there will be a lot of things happening between now and the 20th of January. A lot of things.*"

It is interesting that, in 2016, the left-wing swamp denizens were pushing "Russia, Russia, Russia" election interference. They were the ones yelling fraud, even though they could associate Russia with social media propaganda – and that propaganda was revealed in those districts that went overwhelmingly to Hillary Clinton. It was a reality that inferred Russia wanted Hillary, or that their process was grossly incompetent and not a threat to anyone.

Think about Trump's style. He utilizes sales techniques that are proven to work. His MAGA slogan originated with the highly successful "*Let's Make America Great Again*" call for support that won Reagan his election. The infamous "Wall" is an improvement on Senator Obama's 2006 Secure Fence Act – a tall steel slat fence to replace the flimsy, easily passed, wire and car barriers installed by President Obama and Vice President Biden. And the Obama fence was the same idea that the Democrats wanted and Reagan opposed in 1980.

Democrats – more specifically, California and New York City Democrats – opposed Trump's wall because it would actually work and that would stop them gerrymandering the population numbers they wanted to enhance because it gave them more representation in the House – Trump has come out opposed to gerrymandering and specifically opposed to having undocumented individuals counted in the census numbers and then used to determine House representation.

Trump routinely pushes for the purpose or meaning behind the law. Doing so had gotten him the massive tax breaks associated with the construction of the Trump Tower. But then, we hear that NYC is attempting to find grounds to prosecute him for obedience to various accepted legal practices associated with the real estate industry.

A dim-witted New York District Attorney is seeking Trump's tax records and claiming that he inflated the value of properties to obtain loans and deflated them for property tax purposes.

The dim-wit political publicity seeker does not understand (or trusts his voters/audience does not understand) that real estate is valued in three distinct ways: For insurance, replacement value – the cost to physically rebuild the structure; for mortgages, the value is based on the capitalization of revenues – the equivalent amount of Treasury Notes or other interest-bearing deposits that would return the same revenue; for property taxes, it's fair market value – what a willing buyer would pay a willing seller.

Each method yields a different value. Mortgage companies are interested in the revenue that would be used to repay the loan. As a result, they are only concerned with cashflow. If the interest on a bond is 1%, a $1,000 revenue requires $100,000; if the rate is 10%, only $10,000 is required. However, it might cost $200,000 to replace a property that is destroyed – which would be the insurance value. At the same time, a sale may only yield $75,000, and that would be the property tax basis.

So we have three real-world valuation methods that the New York guys are too dumb to understand and show their actions are consistent with sufferers of Trump Dementia Syndrome {TDS}.

Even as the transition of power has begun, TDS persists in the nonsensical idea TRUMP would step out of character to violate the constitution and law, destroy both his legacy and potentially highly positive place in the history books, by not leaving the White House.

Strategically, Trump's usual negotiation technique requires he hand Biden a booming economy and Stock Market – even with the March crash, the DJIA and S&P500 are ending November at record high levels that are roughly 70% above those he inherited from Obama-Biden in 2016.

In terms of conventional economic indicators, he achieved what Obama "experts" said would be impossible or take a miracle.

Then we had the pandemic – yet, after a brief bear market that now seems to have been more of a correction, or adjustment for the realities of 21st commerce, we see only unemployment due to the lockdowns and constraints of social distancing endure.

In terms of the Coronavirus, Trump had promised a vaccine by the end of the year – and again, the "medical experts" said it was impossible and would take a miracle. Now there are three vaccines ready for distribution in December. Assuming they are effective and people are willing to accept the usual temporary vaccine side-effects, Covid-19 could effectively vanish by July 2021, and Biden would be gifted with an economy that has returned to the upward trajectory established by Trump.

As MSM has reported, Trump is already considering a second run for election in 2024. To ensure that possibility is viable, he must give Biden a perfect situation – one that Biden-Harris can then screwup and, thereby, ensure Trump's place in history as only the second person to hold two POTUS administration titles.

To date, the only President in American history to be elected to two individual terms was Grover Cleveland, POTUS 22&24. It's interesting that prior to the election there was talk phrased in such a way as to infer Trump planned to seek an unconstitutional third term in 2024. As with his refusing to vacate the office, the assertion is irrational and only something a TDS suffer would believe.

However, it might be that Trump understood there was a strong ancestral probability of a loss based on his status as a non-POTUS Cousin – something discussed in previous books and further dealt with in Chapter 5. If that were the case, and given Trump's phrasing habits, he might well have been voicing his intention to repeat the pattern established by Grover Cleveland.

In a Bloomberg article, published on 25 November, entitled *"Joe Biden's Start in the Stock Market Ranks With Any in History"*, there was a chart duplicated here, with my annotated adjustments.

As with many MSM outlets, Bloomberg has taken a positive

view toward Biden and opened the article with the words: "*Good or just lucky, Joe Biden's first three weeks in the stock market have been historically solid ones when measured against newly elected presidents of the past.*"

As we see in the annotation, being "historically solid" is not a true indicator of positive outcomes ahead. Historically, the level of Biden's position is comparable to that of Herbert Hoover, whose first year in office was defined by The Great Depression. And, as the Bloomberg article states: "*It's obviously very early, but the market reality has been the opposite of what Donald Trump predicted for his rival -- a crash.*"

Actually, it was not a Trump prediction, but rather a Trump citation of what Wall Street analysts had said – the full quote being: "*They say the stock market will boom if I'm elected. If he's elected, the stock market will crash.*"

As can assume from the wording, the alternative outcomes that "*will*" occur are events that would follow the inauguration of the respective candidates. Thus the occurrences take place between 2021 and 2024.

In passing, we should also recognize the mention of one of the indicator numbers routinely cited in terms of cycles and patterns of history – 57, the quadrennial cycle of the last term of the Obama-Biden administration.

Here it is credited to Trump: "*Trump made the equity market his report card, and by that measure his grades were exceptional, his administration coinciding with a 57% surge in the S&P 500, the sixth-best for a new administration.*"

On the next page, we see the S&P500 curve throughout the life of the Baby-Boom generation; as shown, the first 40 years of Boomer existence saw a gradual steady rise in value; in the second Reagan term, it became steeper, and then we see the Bush-43 roller coaster that ends with the Great Recession.

In 2010, Boomer demographics kicked in – they turned 65 and exited the workforce. Obama profited from the demographic shift and, in 2015, the Boomers turned 70 – meaning when they hit maximum retirement benefits at 72, demographics favored Trump and we see a very steep rise that would normally result in a bubble and a rather sharp crash.

But, Trump lucked out. Instead of a bubble bursting, we had a Wuhan Virus, the coronavirus, the pandemic that was structured to cull the Boomers – here China gained by the period in which it had the one-child policy.

When, in 1979, Chinese leader Deng Xiaoping restricted China's population growth by limiting couples to only one child, he changed the demographic structure and focus of the nation in a way that strengthened it – reducing the growth in China's population by an estimated 300 million, which allowed the nation to focus on its economic growth. It also created a male bias in births.

This led to an easing of the policy in 2013, and its end in 2015 – again, when the first of the surviving Chinese Baby-Boomers were turning 70. I use the term "surviving" because before 1995 Chinese life expectancy was below 70.

The one-child policy also created a mindset that is common in the Industrialized world. The poor have children, the upwardly mobile-only have one or two children and, for the rich, it becomes an emotional choice that often includes adoption. Phrased another way, per thousand women at opposite ends of the household income spectrum, those in poverty have 50-percent more children. As we move up the household income scale, the number of children per thousand women decreases.

The Baby-Boomers are often referred to as the wealthiest in American history, thus they gave rise to the Baby-Bust. In China, a government-imposed Baby-Bust had the effect of redirecting public energy and resources to amassing wealth.

In the United States, the anti-abortion faction is effectively trying to impose poverty on the masses. If their goal was really pro-life, you would see them pushing for both Universal Healthcare and a Universal Basic Income. Such an approach is logical.

The healthcare to ensure that mother and child are healthy and the basic income to ensure mother and child could live safely while having the added benefit of eliminating what is an extremely bureaucratic and expensive welfare system.

As we have seen with the pandemic stimulus package, when

money is introduced at the base level, both sales and savings result. We see the result in the quick return to employment and the record levels achieved in the various financial markets.

Universal Basic Income {UBI} and Universal Healthcare {M4A} both work. Because they work, Nancy Pelosi and Chuck Schumer dedicated themselves to making the second round of PPP cash unattainable by connecting it to unrelated programs and levels of pork that are unpalatable to the Senate Republicans. And by doing so, they are setting the stage for a failed Biden Presidency.

But the Republicans also realized that withholding Payroll Protection Program money would doom Biden's Administration and the Democratic position in 2024.

In an ideal, Biden supporting, political environment, the goal would be to pass a clean stimulus package that puts money in hands of those who are still unemployed or on Social Security.

The effect would be to stimulate the economy during the Christmas Shopping Season – 2019, retail sales surpassed a trillion dollars; therefore, if we consider salaries and manufacturing profits, the Christmas retail period is momentarily identical to the first stimulus package.

The reported average household spending during the three weeks before Christmas 2019 was $1,536. The stimulus was worth $1,200 plus an added weekly benefit to those unemployed by the pandemic.

Pelosi has made it clear she will not provide any assistance before Christmas. As a result, on 20 January, Joseph Robinette Biden Jr. will assume the Oval Office with an economy denied its Christmas profits.

Since Biden will inherit an economy in which Disneyland is laying off 32,000 theme park workers, Movie Houses are closing – in part because Hollywood cannot produce pictures in a pandemic environment – and top brand retailers are faced with the specter of pandemic induced bankruptcies – JRB faces the awkward position of having a "Great Recession" without the normal economic forces usually associated with a recession.

In a normal recession, the stimulus would be to provide the retail operation with funds needed to retain employees. But in this pandemic environment, the employees and customers must social distance and avoid confined spaces. Retail sales can continue, but only if the customer has the funds to engage in online purchases.

For the film industry, this would seem to mean moving to in-home rentals of first-run productions while competing with various subscription broadcast services – NetFlix, Hulu, etc – who already have entered the "original content" market and include that content in their base subscription price.

American has entered a new age of commerce and Biden will be the first POTUS to deal with its emerging realities. At the same time, his own party is working against him by playing 20th-century politics in an emerging 21ts-century world.

But then, as we know after four years of MSM reporting on Trump, and the impeachment nonsense, we are deeply rooted in the reality of reality avoidance.

Lyndon Baines Johnson {LBJ} experienced an earlier version of "Trump Treatment" and commented on it through a hypothetical example: *"If one morning I walked on top of the water across the Potomac River, the headline that afternoon would read 'President Can't Swim.'"*

The MSM survives by attacking. It will seek to undermine the nation – as we saw with the idea that Trump would refuse to vacate the White House after the election has been certified. We are also hearing that he will petty and snub Biden by refusing to attend the inauguration.

It would certainly be a godsend for the anti-Trump media, but it would also doom any chance of a 2024 run and erase all the positives the history books will present about the Trump legacy. Or, as LBJ phrased it: *"While you're saving your face, you're losing your ass."*

There is no face-saving in appearing petty. Though it can be said that MSM would love it if the target of their attacks gave a solid example of pettiness. Remember, Biden had said he would not claim victory prior to certification of the results. And the media is filled with attacks on Trump because he will not concede defeat prior to certification of the votes and the Constitutional deciding vote by the Electors.

Both men agreed on using the same coin in the electoral toss.

It is MSM that wants to use a different standard and call the election while the coin is still in the air.

Of course, The Trump Card series, in conjunction with the 2017 book, *Jonathon's POTUS Cousins*, called the election before it was held. In effect, it called it before the nominating process had been completed – as is seen on the chart on the back cover of the eighth book in this series, published March, "*2020 IMPEACH V HISTORY*".

When it comes to being President, a POTUS Cousin always defeats a non-cousin, and when two non-cousins compete, it is the one who is descended from the 4-Sisters who will win. In the race between Trump and Biden, both are descendants of the 4-Sisters, but JRB had the advantage of also being a POTUS Cousin, as well as being in the line of three sisters, where DJT is only related to two of them.

However, both men show there was power involved – JRB won with the most votes in the nation's history, while DJT garnered the most votes of any incumbent President. Together, the two men closed the 58th-quadrennial of American history on a high note that the MSM struggled to make flat.

MSM is functioning to implement a variation on another one of LBJ's observations: "*If you can convince the lowest white man he's better than the best colored man, he won't notice you're picking his pocket. Hell, give him somebody to look down on, and he'll empty his pockets for you.*"

They successfully succeeded in having 80 million voters look down on Trump. But their actions had a consequence on the Saudi approach to an Israel agreement.

Over the Thanksgiving weekend, there was a report that the "*Saudi Crown Prince pulled back from normalization with Israel in part because of US election results.*"

While Crown Prince Mohammed bin Salman is eager to build ties with the Biden administration, he was reluctant to act before Biden legally takes office. Strategically, any deal made later would serve to cement relations with the new Administration. Plus, as discussed in Chapter 5, there are other forces at work with regard to the Iranian nuclear weapons program – which is a direct threat to the Saudis.

There is the additional issue of the Saudis repeatedly haven stressed the importance of full normalization of its relations with Israel. However, such a significant Middle eastern peace deal or alliance has a price, and for the Saudis, it is an establishment of the Palestinian state and a Palestinian Authority peace deal with Israel. A Biden problem will also affect the predicted 2033 Middle Eastern war that triggers a global nuclear confrontation.

Joseph Robinette Biden Jr and Kamala Devi Harris no share a platform that will determine the "prophetic" fate of the world as it appears in Biden's Catholic scripture. Will he make America Great? And where did the idea that America's "greatness" had slipped come from?

We know Reagan and Trump used variations on the same MAGA slogan to promote the idea that America needed to be made great again, but we need to, once again, turn to LBJ for the origin of the concept: *"That bitch of a war killed the lady I really loved – the Great Society."*

Endless wars, which Trump has sought to bring to an end, are what made *"the Great Society"* less than great – but MAGA is an easier slogan, and somewhat less vague, than "Make *the Great Society* Great Again."

Then too, with the division in the nation and within the two political parties, we might recall the words: *"Victory is no longer a truth. It is only a word to describe who is left alive in the ruins."*

And as much as I've enjoyed comparing Nixon to Biden, there is the reality that I would like to be wrong where Johnson was right: *"He's [Nixon] like a Spanish horse, who runs faster than anyone for the first nine lengths and then turns around and runs backwards. You'll see; he'll do something wrong in the end. He always does."*

After all, we are stuck with Biden having bragged about his *quid pro quo* blackmail to effectively save Burisma from the work of Ukraine's Prosecutor General.

However, even allowing for possible "voter fraud" and

various improprieties, the majority of voters in California, and therefore in the nation, have decided they would ignore the proven criminality – the self-confessed criminality – in Biden that they sought to charge Trump with through the correct inference that Biden would be his opponent.

It will be a problem for President Biden. To distract from his actions, both House and Senate Republicans will have little choice but to divert time and resources to attacks on the former President and various members of the Trump family.

As a true POTUS Cousin, we can expect Tiffany Trump will be immune from those attacks. As a best selling author, whose books targeted those who will be leading the attacks, we can expect those whose political careers now rest on claims of Trump criminality to redirect millions of taxpayer dollars to wasteful and pointless effort to somehow justify their established lies.

They will keep touting the wondrous truth and beauty of *"The Emperor's New Clothes"* and those who do not wish to appear the fools they really are will accept the lies and continue to see all that which is not there – the *"Overwhelming Evidence"* of crimes that cannot be, and have not been, defined in law.

Harris-Biden has a problem, while California and New York Democrats pursue wasteful retaliation against Trump for having achieved what they asserted was "impossible" or "take a miracle", the national economy will still need to recover from the pandemic mistakes of those same states and individuals.

The problems have already begun – Satan seems to have cast his vote. Curiously, that vote was not against either Biden or Trump – it was to see who would voluntarily step forward and declare a hatred for the nation. Who aligns with those boldly yelling *"Death to America"*?

As Obama told Peter Hamby in a 1 December interview: *"You lost a big audience the minute you say it, which makes it a lot less likely that you're actually going to get the changes you want done. The key is deciding, do you want to actually get something done, or do you want to feel good among the people you already agree with?"*

As Obama pointed out, saying *"defund the police"* might be

a "snappy" slogan, but it only speaks to those who profit from less police protection. In the real world, it has the effect of turning away both voters and would-be supporters.

It could be that the *"defund the police"* related words and deeds are what cost the Democrats House seats. It could also be that the traditional Democrats oppose incessant claims of Trump's wrong-doing when it has repeatedly been shown his fundamental positions are more often than not correct. While he is not a doctor or medical expert, he did say there would be a vaccine before the end of 2020 – and by 2 December, while America rolled out three vaccines, in Russia they had a fourth vaccine they were ready to use on their military.

Trump has claimed voter fraud, and on 1 December, Attorney General William Barr formally stated it occurred – but, while the Justice Department investigations were ongoing, *"to date, we have not seen fraud on a scale that could have effected a different outcome in the election."*

Even though Trump will be proved correct, as discussed in Chapter 5, Satan's Vote or some other historic force ensures us that the fraud will not change in the outcome of the Presidential vote. It is somewhat comical that a Trump-sponsored recount uncovered an additional 87 Biden votes.

in his statement, Barr said: *"Most claims of fraud are very particularized to a particular set of circumstances or actors or conduct. ... And those have been run down; they are being run down. Some have been broad and potentially cover a few thousand votes. They have been followed up on."*

With a margin of six million California votes as the basis for Biden's popular vote majority, a few thousand seem meaningless.

But consider what a few thousand votes on the same ballot would mean in local elections and the passage of local initiatives. If only to ensure local voters get what they honestly voted for, ballots must be valid and honest. And that is what Trump is really fighting for. Bad actors should not swap local or regional laws or mandates.

Harris-Biden has a problem. Do they either stand for honest and fair elections – or not?   And will they catch and correct the flaws in the current election so that, in the next pandemic, they are not an issue?

Then too, their administration might well be called upon to explain the realities inferred from the chart I randomly stuck in at the end of Chapter 1.

It's a basic simple chart. How many deaths per year did we have in the decade between 2009 and 2019? What percentage of the population died?

Knowing those numbers, and allowing for all the disruption caused by Covid-19, how many more people died relative to the 0.71-0.87 percent of the population (0.83-percent average) that would have died anyway?

The highest two years (0.87%) were 2017 and 2018. The Baby-Boomers turned seventy in 2015, and with an anticipated life expectancy of 76.6 for an American male, that could up-tick could reflect World War II babies or those early Baby-Boomers who were raised to be smokers. As the chart shows, there was a sharp drop in 2019 deaths.

The reported Coronavirus deaths would, if they were due to Covid-19, mean the anticipated 2020 deaths would be that much higher than the decade of statical fact – or about fully 1-percent of the currently estimated 332 million Americans. Over three million need to have died in 2020 before the Covid-19 could be called a real pandemic and not a media hoax based on a culling virus whose only purpose is to expedite the deaths of those who were to die anyway within the calendar period.

I know. Many will have an emotional reaction to the idea they were conned. Or, maybe, to the suggestion that death a few months earlier – especially for those confined to long-term nursing facilities – is something to be bemoaned.

People do not like the idea of euthanasia; they especially hate it when it is done by a virus. But, they aren't likely to have been reading this book series. They are more likely in the streets pulling down statues or throwing chairs and bricks through store windows.

CHAPTER FOUR – Culling Effect
"It is difficult to get a man to understand something when his salary depends upon his not understanding."
- Upton Beall Sinclair (1878-1968)

Pandemics are interesting and deadly – if it is a true deadly pandemic. But, as I have repeatedly stated, Coronavirus is a culling virus. If you want to see a deadly one, look at 1918.

The 1918 flu was both real and truly deadly for all those infected. In medical terms, it was the *Big One*, and quickly killed about 675,000 Americans of the estimated 100 million population – a third of those deaths were in a single month, and they were in all age groups.

Covid-19 has taken about ten months to kill 324,473 out of a population of 332 million – and the bulk of the deaths were Baby-Boomers the Silent Generation suffering from other life-threatening medical issues. They certainly were not meandering through the population and having a huge demographic impact – in terms of age or medical condition – since they (we) already reached our age of natural expiration.

In 1919, the Red Cross spread the slogan *"wear a mask, save your life,"* and nurses began to make gauze masks for public use. Gauze isn't the "ideal material', it's too porous, but it is superior to the alternative of no protection. Thus, they were mandated along the East Coast and anyone violating the mandate was prosecuted for "sanitary infractions."

Since the "Spanish Flu" belonged to the First World War, the wearing of a mask was a patriotic gesture consistent with the era.

There is something to consider that has not been spoken of, nor is it likely to be recognized – it smacks of the idea of "destiny," but is purely demographics. That is, people have a time to die, and the annual number of deaths has risen as the first Baby-Boomers passed the age of 70. In this same period, the Baby-Bust has caused the median population age to increase.

Look at the numbers. We know the population and annual deaths since the start of the Obama-Biden administration, in 2009. Throughout the Obama-Biden administration the death rate grew from 0.80% of the population to 0.85%. Throughout that period, the median age grew from 37.2 to 37.9.

The first two years of the Trump administration saw a small increase to 0.87%. But note: in 2015, the Baby-Boomers turned 70 and we expected an upturn in the number of older Americans who died. In 2019, the death rate dropped significantly – from 0.87 to 0.71 or by nearly 20% – and the median age increased sightly or by about 1%.

In terms of Life Expectance or longevity, there has been no demographic change that could not, objectively, be seen as anything but positive – if we assume the following fact reflects a period when people lived longer under Trump than under Obama-Biden.

In 2019 there were 387,380 fewer deaths than were expected based on the Obama-Biden average. As we know, in 2020 Covid-19 culled the older generation so that, by the first of November there were 236,471 deaths attributed to it – which would annualize out to about 283,765 or about 103,615 fewer than the calculated shortfall in 2019. That is to say, over hundred-thousand Americans will be living longer than they would have based on the Obama era casualty numbers. But it will be 2022 before we have accurate causality numbers to evaluate.

The CDC data indicates, after three full years of the Trump administration, many individuals are living longer than expected; to understand the exact reason involves looking at changes in all the causality categories, changes in lifestyle, and then we must address the possibility that changes in medications or medical procedures are artificially extending longevity. Or, it could be that, as Boomers turned 70, they went to the doctor more regularly and caught health problems while they were still in a treatable stage. Increased care is a benefit of Social Security Medicare (or universal Healthcare).

There is also a possibility the Obama-era numbers represent the pre-war Silent Generation dying off.

Regardless of any academic reasoning, the median age of the population is increasing because Baby-Boomers comprise a larger percentage of the population. But that also means death rates will again increase.

By comparison, in 1900 the population was 76,094,000; the life expectancy for a man (based on if the were Black or White) was 33-47; it wasn't until 1953 that the average man could expect to live long enough to collect a full year of Social Security Benefits, and as soon as they could expect more than five years of benefits, the age of full retirement was raised to 70.

In case the numbers have not sunk in.

Social Security, which was originally designed in Germany to be a taxation scam – the idea was to have people willingly donate money to the government for benefits they would, statistically, be unlikely to collect.

That old con-job was carried forward into "The New Deal" and signed into law in 1935 when the life expectancy for men was 60 and 64 for women – the retirement age was set at 65 to ensure that most men, who were the primary workers, would never collect, and their wives were unlikely to collect for more than a few years.

As we know, the Social Security Trust Fund is nothing more than paper – the money is invested in Federal Treasury Notes and the cash is spent by the Government. It was an ideal scheme – until the average male Baby-Boomer lived beyond 65 and his wife lived six years longer.

According to CDC numbers, In 1950 the average male lived to be 65.6 years and a woman 71.1 years. As long as the population was growing and the workforce expanding, the actuarial numbers allowed the con to continue.

But, in 1980, when Ronald Reagan was running for office, we began to hear Social Security was going broke – women were living to 77.4 and men to 70 – and in 1983 the age for full benefits was incrementally raised to 67 with a provision to start early retirement at 62, with 70% benefits, or as late as 70 with a benefit premium that raises the yield to 124%.

What that means, in terms of the con, is that: If you willingly forgo collecting 70% of benefits for eight years, you would be able to collect 124% of those benefits for a year. Of course, demographic data indicates the first world life expectancy in 1983 was 78.1 – but that includes the European nations and serves only to assist in selling the con. To perpetuate the con, Reagan and Congress lied to you – and America bought it.

There is a similar fraud involved when detractors are heard yelling "socialism" or "socialist" when it comes to anything that would help extend lives and therefore undermine the Social Security tax fraud.

The way the fraud was structured, the poorest pay the larger percentage of their income into a system that underwrites the waste that helps make the Military-Industrial Complex type schemes profitable – which helps explain why "Socialist Europe" pays far less for their military, and why they have better retirement plans or basic medical coverage – thus live five or more years longer than the average American, and do so with a standard of living that is arguably equal or superior to that of the United States.

This brings us the issue of Covid-19 and why America seems to be doing worse than other first-world nations.

Based on the 2017 actuarial tables, statistical probability says a man born when Biden was would live until 2029 – assuming a history of good health, which Biden's two brain aneurysms negate.

Since Covid-19 is a culling virus that targets the more sickly elderly, we can expect the death rate relative to population would be decreasing; that explains why the media is focusing on cases rather than deaths – the media motto is "If it Bleeds it Leads." There is no "bleeding" when people are living longer healthier lives.

Any statistic, such as fewer than average deaths yielding a declining overall death rate deprives MSM of the blood it needs for dramatic lead stories. By the same token, the media has a reason to "excuse' or "ignore" BLM violence on any level other than the dramatic pictures of communities burning – they know their prime demographic is the drama demanding morons.

On the Thursday before the election, the Democratic Senate Minority Leader from New York City called President Donald Trump a "moron." But, Senator Charles Ellis "Chuck" Schumer plays to the same demographic as MSM and tabloid journalism – so if he calls the other guy a moron, his base can hold that they, being different, are not the true morons in the story.

Such insults are aimed at the President and the nation, in general; they were not new for Swamp Denizens like Schumer who, along with the habitual liar from California – Congressman Adam Bennett Schiff – like to blame Trump for the actions of those from their respective states who they were relying upon to elect Biden so that Harris could replace him sometime before 2023. That serves to end the POTUS Cousin and 4-Sisters pattern, which then ends the United States' prominence in global affairs.

The day before the election, as part of their misinformation process, House Speaker Nancy Pelosi referred to the coronavirus death toll as "*almost incomprehensible.*"

That is to say, that given the limited mental abilities of her demographic, the idea that half as many people died of the culling virus than die of voluntary tobacco use on an annual basis is "*almost incomprehensible*" because her base demographic is too stupid to comprehend that smoking us far more dangerous than a virus that remains asymptomatic in over 99-percent of those it infects.

Granted, we do not want to carry the virus to those it would kill, and therefore we need to practice social distancing and wear masks. But, Covid-19 is nowhere near the deadliness of the Spanish Flu or any seasonal flu.

According to the CDC, since 2010 the annual death rate that can be attributed to the flu is between 12,000 and 61,000. If we add Covid-19 to the mix, things get more interesting and move further behind the comprehension of demographics supporting Harris-Biden and the Chinese agenda that is synchronized to their 2025 target date – the date they are using for all their major objectives.

This time around, Schumer was asserting the 3rd resurgence of coronavirus cases had seen "*More people are in hospitals, more people are dying. This third wave in the cold weather with the combination of the flu, and we're sitting on our hands and that's because Donald Trump is such a—pardon my saying, I know you have a very nice show—such a moron.*"

Naturally, Schumer was demonstrating willful ignorance or

relying on the presumed ignorance of the electorate, in ignoring the fact that the virus was simply following a globally seen pattern of cyclical emergence. More importantly, he was feeding upon the same nonsense the MSM used in focusing on cases rather than deaths – more significantly excess mortality.

As we covered in book ten and will expand upon here, excess mortality – the number of deaths above those in the same period in prior years – is the only real measure of the seriousness of either a pandemic or natural disaster.

Remember, the 1918 Influenza pandemic saw 675,000 dead with roughly a third – 225,000 – in a single month. Therefore, one month of serious flu is as bad as ten months of Covid-19.

In the ten months before Schumer's disgusting insult to the intelligence of the American voter, Covid-19 had been a cofactor associated with the death of 235,097 Americans, and remember, tobacco kills 480,317 through direct or secondary effects every year. Where is the outrage over tobacco – or is it that Pelosi and Schumer cannot afford to attack the funding they receive from the tobacco industry?

On 16 November, the media was inciting panic – the number of Covid-19 cases had passed the eleven million mark with a million new cases being added in just the preceding seven days. It sounds horrible – out of 11.5 million cases, 250,000 people had died, with nearly 40% of those already suffering from old age disabilities or a medical issue requiring intensive care. Statistically, without Covid-19, they would be still dead in six months to a year.

In contrast to a virus that is generally a passive passenger we know is normally asymptomatic and so is seen only because of mass testing, we have tobacco – which is used by about 40 million adults, plus about 4.7 million middle and high school students. This means about 13.5% of the population is voluntarily consuming a substance that annually kills ten-percent of them – paying roughly $2000 a year for the privilege of being part of a death or debilitation lottery.

Based on the Federal Minimum Wage, they work as much as 275 hours for the right to play a 10% death lottery. Yet, the same people are upset to the point of disrupting the culture over a 2.2% lottery that requires old-age or some potentially fatal illness before playing.

The CDC statistics show that about 1600 kids under the age of 18 will light-up their first cigarette every day – they start playing the death lottery.

Sit in your car in the parking lot of a shopping mall where they say you should wear a mask. Count the number of workers who, when it is time for their break, go outside, remove their mask or face-shield, and light-up a cigarette – a rational incongruity which might explain why they hold a minimum wage job. But their action does serve a practical purpose. After they light-up and have taken a few puffs, take a walk downwind from them.

Do you smell the smoke?

If you can smell the smoke, you have a good idea of how far a virus can travel in a supportive airflow – not the dead air in a store, where the 6-12 foot rule makes sense, but rather the location where there is a fan or air circulation system forcing air to move. It is why you need to wear the filtering mask. And remember, in dead air, the particles are floating and will be moved as people pass – as you pass. You don't want to be in smoke-filled rooms or in a closed space with people who have colds, the flu, or are Covid-19 carriers.

Thus, in the first ten months of 2020, we can safely state that smoking contributed to the death of about 440,000 people, with about 10% from secondhand smoke – fully 30% more than Covid-19.

Those who died from a primary intake of the tobacco smoke and contaminants paid about $2,000 per year to commit suicide – they showed no regard for those murdered by secondary smoke.

Globally, about one-in-seven people are smokers – sharing the defining character of being poor, living in developing nations, or among the Europeans hardest hit by Covid-19. In France, which is known for its smoking, only about 25% smoke and they die at the rate of about 200-a-day. Most of the EU nations average around the same. In Sweden, where they shrugged off concerns about Covid-19, only about 7% smoke.

About half of smokers are in Asia. And that could, in part, be a reason why, even though Covid-19 originated in China, there are far fewer deaths in that region of the globe.

One early coronavirus study discovered that the virus has a harder time infecting smokers. Then too, in China, Japan, and other Asian nations, it is common for those with cold symptoms to wear a mask – so the act of wearing a mask fits into social or cultural normality and provides an added bit of preventative focus.

In America, there are people who assert any mandated mask-wearing is an attack on personal freedoms – whereas, in Japan, it is a sign of good manners and respect.

We've seen Trump take an approach comparable to Sweden or Japan within an American context – individuals decide if they wish to wear a mask and his people have pointed out that the act of wearing a mask includes consideration of risk and social distancing.

Of course, Chuck Schumer calls Trump a moron. Yet, Trump contracted the virus and, because, despite his weight, he is healthy, so his body rejected it. Even rallies referred to as superspreader events failed to generate major outbreaks. And in contrast, Biden must hide in his basement and wear a mask even when outside bicycling – because Biden's history of brain aneurysms makes him a prime target for the worst coronavirus outcome.

As stated throughout the 2020 books in this series, Covid-19 is a culling virus that only affects individuals with other recognized or unrecognized deadly health issues. For that reason, its primary victims have been those over the age of 65 – individuals who have reached their genetic expiration date.

For perspective, the epicenter of the pandemic was and, as of his comment, remained New York State – with 33,652 deaths that were attributed to Covid-19. Of those, 23,979 (71.2%) were in New York City – with the majority (7,400 or 31%) occurring in Schumer's birthplace, Brooklyn/Kings County.

Phrasing the moronic conduct reality in yet another way, Schumer's birthplace/residence/borough accounts for more deaths than 42 states – all of whom had less than 6,000 Covid-19 deaths.

New York City (hence New York State) had more deaths than any other state and, if not for the moronic incompetence of Mayor

Bill De Blasio, New York State would have ranked seventh behind Texas (18,507), California (17,615), Florida (16,720), New Jersey (16,470), Illinois (9,994), and Massachusetts (9,975).

At least, that would have been the case based if the multiple University studies citing New York City as the direct cause of more than 65% of the United States cases were in error.

In 2018, the U.S. Death rate was 867.8 per 100,000 people or 2,839,205, Life expectancy: 78.7 years, Infant Mortality rate: 5.66 deaths per 1,000 live births.

The leading causes of death were Heart disease: 655,381, Cancer: 599,274, Unintentional Injury: 167,127, Chronic Respiratory diseases: 159,486, Stroke (cerebrovascular diseases): 147,810, Alzheimer's disease: 122,019, Diabetes: 84,946, Influenza and Pneumonia: 59,120, Nephritis, nephrotic syndrome and nephrosis: 51,386, Intentional self-harm (suicide): 48,344.

It is interesting to note, on 24 November, it was reported that *"Global flu infections hit record lows amid pandemic."* This is interesting and infers that many Covid-19 deaths might be culled cases of the flu or other respiratory problems.

While it was too early for a definitive analysis, globally, the only place showing a high rate of flu transmission was in Southeast Asia – where, on a per capita basis, a significant absence of Covid-19 has been noted. Based on population, both the coronavirus case and death rate should have been in descending order from China, India, and the United States – if we recorded based on national geographic borders. If we simply went by geography – which MSM avoids – the United States would move down the list and below Europe and the European Union.

However, the flu transmission numbers do reveal that nearly 25-percent of Covid-19 deaths were reclassified respiratory deaths that would otherwise have occurred anyway. As other case-of-death tallies are produced, we will see other classifications have lost cases and thus compensate, on a zero-sum-basis for the Covid-19 cases.

Note that the media has made brief or transient mention of the 1918 Spanish Influenza pandemic which killed about a third of the global population – which included about 675,000 Americans of the roughly 76 million recorded in the 1900 census, and 101 million in the 1910 census. In 1920, the census recorded a total population of 172 million in the centennial United States and its possessions. And, even with the Influenza losses, from 1910 to 1920 roughly 14 million were added to the population.

The culling effect seems to be a characteristic shared by all plagues and pandemics. When we look at the overall effect, there is a strange characteristic that differentiates between the personal loss felt by family members and the more impersonal loss to society.

The "impersonal" loss serves to benefit the survivors.

Look at Covid-19, a respiratory disease that has shown to be passive and asymptomatic in well over 90-percent of the cases. Where it causes hospitalization or death, the infected individual has some form of severe medical issue - for those under the age of fifty, it is often undiagnosed until they are being treated for the covid. It can be argued that, in most cases, the Covid diagnosis was the catalyst for treatment of the underlying condition and ultimately saved or extended their lives.

When it comes to issues like Covid or the economy, the *"Our World in Data"* website serves as an excellent source of relevant analysis and documented data. One such analysis is a November 2020 article: *"Breaking out of the Malthusian trap: How pandemics allow us to understand why our ancestors lived in poverty."*

When we view Covid-19, we can play a glass half empty or a glass half full game, or simply thinking *"Yin and Yang"* – two parts or halves of the same structure.

As the article states of the Malthusian trap {also known as the Malthusian catastrophe}: *"For much of human history, there was no escape from poverty. Our ancestors were trapped in an economy in which incomes were determined by the size of the population. Productivity gains did not raise living standards, but instead translated to increases of the population size, which left everyone as badly off as before."*

The concept derives its name from Thomas Robert Malthus who, in 1798, published a book entitled *"An Essay on the Principle of Population"* in which he balanced population growth against food resources and economic prosperity. Part of the thesis proposed that a rising population would have the effect of decreasing wages. Yet another aspect of population growth was that it would outrun the ability to produce food and resources needed to sustain the growing number of people.

Historically, whenever there is a Great Plague or pandemic, the result is an economic benefit to the survivors. One such benefit is a significant increase in real wages. This a period when society escapes the Malthusian trap.

Permanent technological change – such as we are now seeing with the internet, renewable energy, microcircuits, and changes to luminescent fixtures requiring less energy, are all coming together to aspects of the Malthusian premise. But that does not change the reality, and when the Baby-Boomers die, assuming the Baby-Bust continues, there should be a sharp increase in the standard of living.

If Biden introduces a Universal Basic Income and raises both the Minimum Wage and Minimum Social Security so as to eliminate the welfare subsidy, the American standard of living will increase substantially.

The rise in Social Security can easily be funded by removing the cap on income subject to contribution. And, we also need to recognize that the enhanced benefit costs would be short-lived – the Baby-Boomers turn 70 in 2015, and by 2025 the first of them will have passed their expiration date; by 2045, the vast majority of the Baby-Boom generation will have passed into history, with the last of them comfortably over 80-years old.

As with many cycles, the Malthusian trap follows the 49, 57, 60-year cycle patterns. That means, apart from the war due in 2033, the next major change isn't due until 2069 – when the last members of Generation-X pass into history.

The pandemic and resulting stimulus packages have shown potential benefit – a benefit which, if not for the lockdowns and social distancing, would not negatively impact the deficit. On the contrary. If individuals were functioning normally tax revenues would be up significantly, reducing both deficits and debt.

In classical terms, the growth and resulting shortages would then unleash the Four Horseman of the Apocalypse {*1. White Horse; 2. Red Horse, 3. Black Horse; 4. Pale Horse*} – conquest, war, famine, plague – which combine to provide various sources of death across a quarter of the earth's surface. There is no mystical element, the symbolic horses and their riders are simply things that always have gone together.

In terms of the Malthus thesis, we can dd to the bi-product of population growth Global Warming caused by traditional fossil fuel use that increases in tandem with the population – or did until the dawn of renewable energy within the context of modern electronics.

To promote that future, Chicago-based Invenergy announced the start of a $1 billion solar energy site to be completed by 2023. It will create 600 jobs, take 36-months to complete, and produce enough energy to power 300,000 homes.

If Biden does his job and encourages more projects like this, the Green New Deal will make it unnecessary to be part of the Paris Climate Accord and place America well ahead of all other nations.

The Book of Revelation introduces the symbolic horsemen in the conjunction with prophecies or statistical model predictions of a time when the population of ALL life will be reduced by a third.

We are, in terms of Global Warming and various extinctions at that stage in history – which the author of Revelation placed in the current second millennia as dated from the era of the prediction. In March 2014 Amazon published my book, "Biblical Prophecy: Are we in the Revelation Era", which presented the event dating inferred by the use of the 19-year and 57-year cycles of the Hebrew Calendar.

As my readers know, to date, everything has happened on the mathematically derived schedule which sees the White Horseman – the Roman symbol for Germany – as Adolph Hitler and the Nazis; in that context, the prediction of the death of 144,000 Jews would be the Holocaust, which served to conceal that mass death. As we know, three of the horseman are simply forms of death, so we can say the prediction simply said there would be a leader and death.

In the age of Covid-19, the twin forces are propaganda and death, where death is connected to age hand heart health – plus a few other pre-existing conditions which are not normally viewed as medical issues, such as obesity.

Obesity can be connected to Type 2 diabetes and, if you are infected with Covid, will double the risk of death – it's even worse if you have autoimmune-related Type 1 diabetes. Combined, the two forms of diabetes account for a third of all Covid-19 deaths. And both forms of diabetes are connected to obesity and a Body Mass Index (BMI) of 40 or more.

About 10.5% of the U.S. population has diabetes. And among those over 65, that increases to 26.8% – which corresponds to the estimated 30+% death rate. In terms of obesity, in 2020 the United States had an obesity rate of about 36.2%. This placed it about 12th in the world where the top ten are Island nations removed from the commercial spread routes and number 11 is Kuwait which, as of 26 November, had 141,547 cases and 872 deaths among its 4,295,822 population – ranking it 45th among nations and giving it a 3.2% infection rate that was roughly consistent with the USA rate.

Southeast Asia and China (6.2%) have very low obesity rates.

We also have the culling issue of roughly 40% of American Covid deaths being in long-term care facilities. These are not Joe Biden, Nancy Pelosi, or Donald Trump healthy elderly members of society.

Those who have died have been removed from family and friends were under 24/7 nursing supervision. They fall within the group the CDC classifies as being "high-risk" due to their underlying health conditions.

Throughout human history, culture, religion, and therefore mythology, have seen society engaged in the phenomenon of twin motifs. This is visually seen in the Asian circular symbol, Yin and Yang where the two halves of the circular while are defined by an S-shape that changes direction in the exact middle of the circle.

Western cultures draw a straight line through the center of the pie and, in our charts, have the line radiate from the center to the edge with each segment unequal and different.

Within western culture this can be seen to attack what is the common element of all cultures -- that of the twin mythological heroes of forces symbolized by heaven and hell, or life and afterlife, the solar and lunar in which the forces of light control the day while invading the dark. One twin or brotherly force might slay the other as Cain did Able, or it dominates in the manner of Romulus over Remus. It might even be such that we forget about the second, as in the case of Hercules and his half-brother Iphicles.

In the current evolutionary era, the twin forces take several forms: America v China; Trump v Biden; Republican v Democrat.

Culturally, we have race or gender domination and control -- makes dominating females in all things, while we see people saving a bible that says the male dominates the fields while the wife has dominion in the home and overall things pertaining to it.

In the universe of Yin and Yang, there is equality and unity. Yet, in western culture, the twin stories evolved into tales of conflict and the need for one half to dominate over its natural counterpart. Thus separating the two and rendering both weaker.

Early in this book series, I spoke of Trump's China goal -- the division of the globe between two mercantile powers. China is a classic non-exclusive nation whose borders have been roughly defined for 2500-years. America is a new land that quickly took control of global shipping and the carrying of goods or services around the globe.

While America is a young nation, it's roots are firmly set in the pattern established by Britain. And, when we remember that, we see a nation whose commerce roots date back before the time of Caesar -- who, when his forces reached Britain, marveled at the ships that could sail against the wind. Curiously, Caesar could not grasp that, to sail against the wind, you must be willing to harness the true nature of the wind.

We are stepping into the next phase in history, the one in which the Bible predicted a third of life would die – and in which we are watching a third of humanity that is the Baby-Boom reaching its natural expiration while climate change caused by the classic activities of humanity is creating the basis for mass extinctions and a new cycle of species evolution.

We can oppose it, then become extinct, or accept it and evolve into the species whose biblical dictate is to care for the planet.

Under Trump, for all his nonsense about promoting fossil fuels, he did suggest the border wall should be a solar array. And when the swamp denizens rejected the idea, that did not stop the border state of Texas from advancing to produce more renewable energy than coal produces energy for the whole nation.

As of November 2020, a new solar array field in Texas has been started – by 2023, it will produce enough energy to power 300,000 homes.

Curious that none of the Paris Climate Accord nations have created a single green energy project of that magnitude. And, if the swamp denizens focused on action feather than meaningless political symbolism, other states in the nation could do what Texas is doing and by the end of Biden's first term, America would be the greenest nation on the planet.

		0	ELECT	P#	INAUGURATE		PRESIDENT	SUCCESSOR
		1	1788	1	30-Apr-1789	1	George Washington	
		2	1792		30-Apr-1793	2		
		3	1796	2	04-Mar-1797	3	John Adams	
1	0	4	1800	3	04-Mar-1801	4	Thomas Jefferson	
		5	1804		04-Mar-1805	5		
		6	1808	4	04-Mar-1809	6	James Madison	
		7	1812		04-Mar-1813	7		
		8	1816	5	04-Mar-1817	8	James Monroe	
		9	1820		04-Mar-1821	9		
		10	1824	6	04-Mar-1825	10	John Quincy Adams	
		11	1828	7	04-Mar-1829	11	Andrew Jackson	
		12	1832		04-Mar-1833	12		
		13	1836	8	04-Mar-1837	13	Martin Van Buren	
2	1	14	1840	9	04-Mar-1841	14	William Henry Harrison	John Tyler
		15	1844	11	04-Mar-1845	15	James K. Polk	
		16	1848	12	04-Mar-1849	16	Zachary Taylor	Millard Fillmore
		17	1852	14	04-Mar-1853	17	Franklin Pierce	
		18	1856	15	04-Mar-1857	18	James Buchanan	
3	2	19	1860	16	04-Mar-1861	19	Abraham Lincoln	Andrew Johnson
		20	1864	17	04-Mar-1865	1	Andrew Johnson	
		21	1868	18	04-Mar-1869	2	Ulysses S. Grant	
		22	1872		04-Mar-1873	3		
		23	1876	19	04-Mar-1877	4	Rutherford B. Hayes	
4	3	24	1880	20	04-Mar-1881	5	James A. Garfield	Chester A. Arthur
		25	1884	22	04-Mar-1885	6	Grover Cleveland	
		26	1888	23	04-Mar-1889	7	Benjamin Harrison	
		27	1892	24	04-Mar-1893	8	Grover Cleveland	
		28	1896	25	04-Mar-1897	9	William McKinley	
5		29	1900	26	04-Mar-1901	10	Theodore Roosevelt	
		30	1904		04-Mar-1905	11		
		31	1908	27	04-Mar-1909	12	William Howard Taft	
		32	1912	28	04-Mar-1913	13	Woodrow Wilson	
		33	1916		04-Mar-1917	14		
6	4	34	1920	29	04-Mar-1921	15	Warren G. Harding	Calvin Coolidge
		35	1924	30	04-Mar-1925	16	Calvin Coolidge	
		36	1928	31	04-Mar-1929	17	Herbert Hoover	
		37	1932	32	04-Mar-1933	18	Franklin D. Roosevelt	
		38	1936		20-Jan-1937	19		
		39	1940		20-Jan-1941	1		
		40	1944		20-Jan-1945	2		Harry S. Truman
		41	1948	33	20-Jan-1949	3	Harry S. Truman	
		42	1952	34	20-Jan-1953	4	Dwight D. Eisenhower	
		43	1956		20-Jan-1957	5		
7	5	44	1960	35	20-Jan-1961	6	John F. Kennedy	Lyndon B. Johnson
		45	1964	36	20-Jan-1965	7	Lyndon B. Johnson	
		46	1968	37	20-Jan-1969	8	Richard Nixon	
		47	1972	38	20-Jan-1973	9		Gerald Ford
		48	1976	39	20-Jan-1977	10	Jimmy Carter	
8		49	1980	40	20-Jan-1981	11	Ronald Reagan	
		50	1984		20-Jan-1985	12		
		51	1988	41	20-Jan-1989	13	George H. W. Bush	
		52	1992	42	20-Jan-1993	14	Bill Clinton	
		53	1996		20-Jan-1997	15		
9		54	2000	43	20-Jan-2001	16	George W. Bush	
		55	2004		20-Jan-2005	17		
		56	2008	44	20-Jan-2009	18	Barack Obama	
		57	2012		20-Jan-2013	19		
		58	2016	45	20-Jan-2017	1	Donald Trump	
10		59	2020	46	20-Jan-2021	2	Joseph R. Biden	Kamala Harris
		60	2024	47	20-Jan-2025	3		
		61	2028	48	20-Jan-2029	4		
		62	2032	49	20-Jan-2033	5		

WORLD WAR THREE {Apocalypse} starts in Middle East

CHAPTER FIVE – Probabilities
"If we ask you to stay home we should also send you money so you can do so."
~ Andrew Yang, Tweet, Wed, 18 Nov 2020

Among probabilities is a certainty – old guard politicians are not interested in the people they supposedly represent.

Prime examples of the thesis are seen in Nancy Pelosi, Chuck Schumer, Andrew Cuomo, and Bill De Blasio. Whether or not Joe Biden is one of their numbers remains uncertain until he has taken occupancy of the Oval Office.

However, Biden did run on a platform based on a declaration that he wasn't Trump. And some of the things we know, factually, about Trump is that he opposed endless wars – as Ivanka Trump tweeted on 18 November:

"When @realDonaldTrump took office, 12,966 military members were serving in Afghanistan & 7,538 were in Iraq. By Jan. 15, American troop presence will be reduced to 2,500 in Afghanistan & 2,500 in Iraq. President Trump is ending the endless foreign wars. God Bless our troops!"

Not being Trump, will Biden seek to emulate another zero-year POTUS, George W, Bush, and accelerate the combat?

Or will he engage in something like zero-year POTUS Ronald Reagan in 1985 and institute his version of the Iran-Contra affair, when *"Senior administration officials secretly facilitated the sale of arms to the Khomeini government of the Islamic Republic of Iran, which was the subject of an arms embargo"*?

Iran's nuclear program is on the table.

Under Obama, Iran was allowed to continue all the necessary research, providing there was no non-research related stockpiling of fissionable material before 2025. That year also happens to be the target year for China to have only renewable energy vehicles and to otherwise be on track to energy independence within the context of the needs of its New Silk Road initiative to dominate global trade.

As we know, Trump didn't like the idea that China would

become the world's mercantile power and has acted accordingly; he also objected to Iran developing nuclear weapons technology. As we know, under the Obama agreement, after 2025, Iran would be free to deploy nuclear weapons. Since Biden is not Trump, we can expect him to permit or even encourage Iran to turn to the Chinese puppet state of North Korea for technological assistance, while the Chinese move to further enhance their global mercantile status – while also receiving oil from Iran.

On the Friday following Thanksgiving, Iran was again in the news after the senior Iranian nuclear scientist, Muhsin Fahrizadeh was assassinated. On Sunday, Iran's Parliament voted to lift the rate of uranium enrichment to 20% – a functional nuclear weapon level of enrichment.

MP Mohammad Bagher Ghalibaf, speaking for The National Security Committee of the Iranian parliament, announced the vote and commented: "*I hope our decision will put an end to the nonsense and terrorism that our enemies are promoting.*" Words which echo the mentality of Mayor De Blasio and Governor Cuomo blaming Trump for their actions in handling the pandemic.

The early appearance of the Chinese Covid-19 in Iran shows a close ongoing commercial relationship between the two nations. It follows that China would likely facilitate an exchange of nuclear technology between North Korea and Iran.

If Biden assists, his actions would enhance the probability of a Third World War in 2033 – that would then complete the Biblical Revelation timeline laid out in my 2014 book, "*Biblical Prophecy: Are we in the Revelation Era*".

In terms of China's control of the mercantile community, it is worth recalling that they provide about 90-percent of our medical needs, and a sizable portion of our electronic technology – phones, laptop computers. Etc.

China also dominates the CBD Industry – CBD, cannabidiol, a compound derived from hemp and cannabis plants that serve as a dietary supplement. Because Federal Law still opposes many of the uses for cannabis – because marijuana is illegal on the Federal level – America has ceded control of the industry to China. It has been projected that, by 2022, the CBD Industry alone will exceed $22 Billion in sales.

Various other cannabis-related products have far broader market potential and a projected growth rate of 20-percent per year with the overall market reaching $80 billion. But, again, that's in a market being hampered by the mindset that gave us prohibition, and yet allows the United States to represent 90-percent of the global marijuana market while foregoing participation in a broader market.

As of 2020, twelve elections were held in a year that ended in Zero. Of those eight saw the elected President replaced by their Vice President. And of those five were due to the death of the President, and all occurred after a non-descendant of the 4-Sisters occupied the Oval Office. Therefore, reducing the numbers to the initial election, we find there were five deaths out of five years that ended in zero where the year was also the one in which the individual was elected.

The chart on the following page shows all of the presidents when they were first elected, the vice president who replaced them, and the date of their inauguration. It also shows the quadrennial cycle.

Earlier books in this series have been identified the 56th or 57th quadrennial relationship to a Metonic calendar use of 19 as it appears in Stonehenge and both the Hebrew and Chinese calendars.

Zachary Taylor, who was not elected in a zero year, died of natural causes; FDR, the zero-year was his third elected term and he also died of natural causes after being elected to his fourth term; Richard M. Nixon was not elected in a zero-year and his resignation was directly related to pending criminal charges emerging from the Watergate break-in.

The mention of Nixon only has relevance because he was replaced by his Vice President, Gerald Ford, who had also replaced the elected Vice President, Spiro T. Agnew – who was convicted of criminal conduct.

As seen on the chart at the beginning of this chapter, there were ten instances when a president was first elected in a zero-year, the most recent being Joe Biden's; five of those presidents died in office, and two survived to be elected to a second term.

Thomas Jefferson, the first to be elected in a zero-year, served without incident; Ronald Reagan was also elected in a zero-year and, 69-days after his inauguration at the age of 69, and 52-days after his 70th birthday, he was wounded in an assassination attempt by John Hinckley Jr.; the twelfth POTUS, Zachary Taylor, and the thirty-second, Franklin D. Roosevelt, also died in office, but since their first term was not the result of a zero-year election, their deaths mean there is a 7 in 44 {16%} chance of a President dying in office.

However, for those Presidents who are initially elected in a zero-year, the probability of dying in office appears to be 5 in 9 or about 55.5%. So it's roughly even money that Joseph R Biden will not survive his first-term. But, that's simply based on history; the real question is how he even managed to be elected. As we will see, that accomplishment reflects the POTUS Cousin 4-Sisters effect – which will also save his life and generally protect him.

We know Biden publically confessed to blackmailing a foreign head of state in violation of 18USC – where subsequent evidence in the form of his son's business laptop and thousands of incriminating emails shows millions of dollars in personal gain in the form of bribes laundered through businesses owned by his son Hunter and other family members. Voters were also aware that Hunter Biden's laptop contained thousands of emails constituting far more damaging evidence than anything that existed against Nixon when the Watergate break-in was the focus of Presidential criminal acts.

Of course, the self-provided overwhelming evidence of Biden improprieties did not interfere with the mail-in ballots and early voting which preceded the revelation of Hunter Biden's hard drive and the thousands of emails detailing his father's cut of the family proceeds. Nor were voters deterred by detailed objectives related to Burisma and other "pay-for-play" operations which had made Joe Biden wealthy.

America voted and declared its devotion to and desire for a self-confessed criminal in the Oval Office. But this reality that was becoming evident when Book-10 was being written. Biden was and shall remain *"Above the Law."*

Or, as pointed out on the closing pages of Book-10:

"Biden can boast of violating Federal Laws; he can claim Trump never mentioned whatever – even while there are videos of Trump elaborating on the topic. Biden tells 85% of the people he is going to raise their taxes. The rich will keep their "loopholes" and deductions.

"The Emperor's New Clothes are seen and accepted, shall we assume the Harris Administration begins on 20 January 2021?"

Why the "Harris Administration"?

Because that's how both Biden and Harris termed it, and because the historic odds are that Biden will die in office. Of course, Pelosi might pressure Biden to resign for health reasons, though a 2022 change in control of the House could bring about a Nixon-type run for the hills.

With Nixon, Spiro Agnew was neither a POTUS Cousin nor a descendant of the 4-Sisters; that meant he could not continue the silent tradition and, therefore, could not rise to the Oval office. Thus Agnew was replaced by Gerald Ford, who was both a POTUS Cousin and a descendant of the 4-Sisters.

Thus, Nixon's resignation occurred only after the continuity of tradition was assured. Those who have read *Jonathon's POTUS Cousins* are aware that, except for her marriage to Bill, Hilary has no connection to the traditional leadership succession.

In *Jonathon's POTUS COUSINS,* I pointed out that, based on the use of 1570 as the ancestor tracing cut-off date, both Hillary and Donald Trump shared the common traits of both not being POTUS Cousins, but had married into the line and produced a daughter who was a POTUS Cousin.

There are marginal similarities between the POTUS Cousins.

Chelsea Victoria Clinton was born in 1980 and in 2014, four years after her marriage to Marc Mezvinsky, had gone on to earn a Doctor of Philosophy in international relations from the University of Oxford in England.

Tiffany Ariana Trump was born in 1993, and in May 2020 received her Doctor of Law degree from Georgetown University Law Center in Washington, D.C.

As an only child, Chelsea doubled up on similarities to the

Trump children. Notably, like Ivana Marie "Ivanka" Trump, who was born in 1981, and married the Orthodox Conservative Jewish, Jared Kushner, Chelsea's husband is a Conservative Jew – whereas Ivanka converted, Chelsea did not. And both girls produced three children.

Vice President-elect, Kamala Harris also married Jewish

As you would have learned in earlier books in this series, by tracing the genealogies back before 1570 it was revealed that all the presidents are descendants of Charlemagne through the 4-Sisters who were born around 1170. Trump is connected to one sister and Biden is connected to both that sister and a second one. Biden is also related to at least twenty-eight other Presidents.

In terms of Presidential Elections, the connection as a POTUS Cousin and how many of the 4-Sisters are in your ancestral line are the factors that seem to control who wins. In a race between a family member and a non-family member, the family member has always won – if only through the Electoral College, as was shown in the narrow margin between George W. Bush and the non-family member, Al Gore.

Now we have Kamala Harris – a first in terms of both gender and race, a female Vice President, and the first Black or Asian to hold the office. As of this writing, Kamala does not appear to be a member of the ancient line dating back to Emperor Charlemagne and the 4-Sisters. What she did have going for her was being 56 in an environment where 56 and 57 are of ongoing significance in the context of historic change.

Since Kamala is not family, we can assert that, in an election where her opponent is family, she cannot win – but Tulsi Gabbard is family and because Republicans have no viable family candidate, Tulsi could win the office in 2024. Her only obstacle would be the possibility that the voters and Electoral College structure might join or align in a manner that ends the century's old tradition and bring down the nation.

If the nation wants to fall, or that is its pre-destined fate, then Biden will die in office, Kamala will become the first female POTUS, and we will need to consider the possibility of a European collapse and an America that is returning to the "Grandpa Was a Deity" roots which are the foundation of all modern cultures and societies.

In other words, it could be a good thing.

Of course, simple leadership genealogy can be carried beyond the limitations of simple ties to noble leadership ancestry. Everyone carries a life pattern that was determined by their parents and the social environment in which they were raised.

In Book-10 I also played with "numerology" – that is, what is a coincidence of numbers in the life of Joe Biden or Donald Trump. As we know, Trump was born in 1946, and the number 46 seems to permeate the life of Joe Biden – who, as of 20 January 2021, will be POTUS-46.

As recounted in Book-10, the number 49 has a long history of numeric and astronomy significance, but, in the case of Joe Biden, there seems to be a pattern of 46 and 47 that holds an important role in the events relating to his life. I'll recount some of them here:

- On 30 May 2015, at the age of 46, Biden's namesake son, Joseph Robinette "Beau" Biden III (born 3 February 1969). died of brain cancer, nearly four months into his 47th year of life.

- At the time of the 2020 election, Beau's widow, Hallie Olivere Biden (born 30 November 1974) was in her 46th year of life.

- Biden was born on 20 November 1942 and 46-years later, in 1988, was operated on for twin brain aneurysms – one in the right hemisphere the other in the left. Those aneurysms are the source of his current verbal and cognitive issues. A third and potentially fatal aneurysm would serve to elevate Kamala Harris to POTUS-47. It would also make Biden the sixth to die having been elected in a zero year.

- While Biden would be designated POTUS-46, he is only the 45th person to hold that office – Grover Cleveland served two separated terms and was, therefore, #22 & #24. The idea was floated about a Trump run for re-election in 2024, implying the desire to duplicate Cleveland's achievement.

- On 7 November 1972, Biden was elected Senator; as the chart shows, his Senate election was a 47th-quadrennial

- election; sworn in on 5 January 1973, 47-years later – exactly 48 years after his first election victory, he was the President-Elect.

- As we know, Trump's campaign cited Biden having achieved less in his 47 years in politics than Trump did in 47-months. If elections have significance, then Biden's victory has served to achieve or at least ensure his place in the history books – though he will need to avoid worsening the economy and restore all the positives achieved by Trump before he can claim any real accomplishments.

- As mentioned, globally, the average male's life expectancy is 70.8; the U.S. – life expectancy of 76.6 – ranks 46th among those nations – it was an age Biden had already exceeded on election day. Meaning he has passed his natural expiration date and is ripe for maintaining the Zero-Year tradition.

- When Barack Hussein Obama was elected POTUS-44, it was interesting that he inherited a war that had been initiated for the purpose of murdering a similarly named head of state, Saddam Hussein. Coincidences are interesting.

- Under Obama, Biden was the nation's 47th Vice President; now Harris is the 49th, where 49 is an OMER count and has a classical significance for the first female Vice President. On 10 August, a poll showed that 57% of unaffiliated voters and 49% of Democrats believed Harris would be elevated to the Oval Office before the 2025 inauguration.

- That poll was several weeks before the 57th anniversary of Martin Luther King, Jr's, "I Have a Dream" speech – given on 23 August 1963. As we know, the election proved to be as messed up as predicted, there is no "final tally." The 57th anniversary of the John F. Kennedy assassination (on 22 November 1963) passed; the Electoral College convened and Biden won. As you might know, and as shown on the chart, 57 is also a significant chronological milestone.

- Looking at Biden's current wife, Jill Biden, between her two husbands she has been married for 47 years and is therefore tracking Biden's political life through her married one. The need to attack also extended to Jill Biden's traditional use of

"Dr." based on her Doctorate – a sexist attack is shown in the fact nobody objected to "Dr." Martin Luther King Jr's use of the term for a "Doctor of Theology", but are attacking "Dr." Jill Biden's academic recognition for holding a "Doctor of Education."

- Our final 47 comes with the prospect of Trump running again in 2024, and a November 2020 poll indicating 47-percent of voters support it. It helps that 75-percent of Republicans had said they support it. In the meantime, we're stuck *'Biden' Our Time* until the new administration reveals any strengths or weaknesses, and if there is a clarity of focus that can grow the economy while putting the Covid-19 bogeyman away.

Given that, before Biden, only 9 of the 45 individuals who became President were elected for the first time the 55.5% zero-year curse will be watched. In terms of Satan's Vote, 2020 was also a Christmas Star year and marked the first time in 800 years that the conjunction of Saturn and Jupiter fell on the Winter Solstice.

There was the attempted assassination of Ronald Reagan; if that is included, the number conforms to a biblical 66.6% event.

Then too, there were three assassination attempts of George W. Bush and that would bring the odds into the 78-percent range. But if we consider all the attempts, we reach a 100-percent chance of something threatening Biden's life.

Based on the probabilities, and factoring in the possibility of Covid-19 exposure when he takes office, with the added element of a blood clot induced brain aneurysm, he could die as early as 20 February 2021, or as late as 23 November 2023.

Based on the standard deviation for the four who lived more than a month after taking office, Biden's death could be as early as 9 October 2021 or as late as 1 May 2024 – his death on or after the average, 20 January 2023, would Constitutionally grant Harris the right to run for two consecutive terms in addition to finishing the Biden term.

However, Biden does have one thing going for him – the fact that he is a POTUS Cousin. As has been the tradition throughout every election since George Washington, when there is a choice to be made, given that both candidates are descendants of the 4-Sisters, the one who is not a POTUS Cousin will lose to the one that is.

Whenever neither is a POTUS Cousin – as with HRC against DJT or the election of Andrew Jackson – the 4-Sisters' descendant will prevail. We can now repeat what these kinship relationships have to do with Biden or any advantage his presidency might enjoy?

As stated, JRB is both a POTUS Cousin and a descendant of the 4-Sisters, while Kamala Harris is neither. What that means is, unless Satan's Vote dictates the United States is to come to an end, Harris cannot be elevated to the Oval Office. Harris is simply not historically qualified – she's neither as a member of American's ruling elite nor related to traditional European Nobility.

Whether or not Biden is truly a qualified member will be seen with the reaction to his urging Congress to pass an economic relief bill before the post-election lame-duck session ends. The problem with that is Trump, who suggested the new package should be $2,000 rather than the original $1,200.

Congress played games and on 21 December – the Winter Solstice and Christmas Star day – was scheduled to finally vote to provide $600. But Satan cast his vote and a combination of printer issues and a computer glitch prevented uploading the bill to the congressional computers.

It wouldn't be until 2 p.m. that the 5,500-page bill would be uploaded carted through the Capitol as what might be the largest Bill in history – combining the stimulus with an omnibus funding Bill called "Consolidated Appropriations Act of 2021."

Neither house of Congress has any interest in the average voter or Presidential leadership. They only want to play games that demonstrate their political power. Their childish behavior shows that the prospects for an economic recovery in 2021 remain slim.

While there was a Bipartisan group of senators preparing the $908 billion stimulus plan, the Schumer-Pelosi partisan logjam is not about to vanish. House Speaker Pelosi is not likely to want to abandon her puppet master role unless or until, as AOC called for, she is removed from power.

For months now, House Speaker Nancy Pelosi has been at odds with President Trump's negotiators and she would rather have seen people starve than give him legislation he can claim as his own.

Pelosi takes enormous delight in serving her Satanic master by playing the Wicked Witch of the West and rallying those forces that can only bring harm to the nation. But she failed on one level – the omnibus Bill has $1.35 Billion for Trump's Wall.

CHAPTER SIX– Challenge to Biden
"handed me a card like the one I have in my pocket with the schedule on it, of all the things I'm gonna do. "
~ Joe Biden

As the year drew to an end, the dating service "Match.com" was running an ad where Satan is matched to a young lady named 20-20. And they seem very happy.

Global politics might be a different form of match-making, and several nations celebrated Biden's victory and Trump's loss. Similar celebrations took place in numerous States.

Russia was quiet about the transition and Iran was looking forward to safely continuing its nuclear weapons research into the year 2025 when it would be free to arm itself to a level comparable to that of North Korea.

Many in the nation welcome the Biden victory because it should put an end to the pointless waste associated with Mueller-style multi-million dollar investigations into Russian collusion that everyone knows was done by Hillary Clinton's team and not Trump.

Since Biden is above the law, there will be no investigations into the evidence of the Obama administration utilizing resources of the FBI to spying on Trump and his campaign. Nor will there be money spent on the Biden *quid pro quo* Ukraine blackmail. Thus we will not be burdened with endless news stories of corruption in Washington.

Biden has set an agenda that involves the creation of "Biden-care" as a replacement for, or augmentation of, Obamacare. While Americans are not likely to see the highly efficient and cost-effective medical care associated with the Australian model that Trump had praised, there may be a return to the tax penalty associated with the ACA mandate.

Biden will also have to contend with whatever SCOTUS rules concerning the constitutionality issue of the 2010 Affordable Care Act in the case which went before the court on 9 November 2020.

In September, Trump stated his belief: "*Obamacare will be replaced with a MUCH better, and FAR cheaper, alternative if it is terminated in the Supreme Court."*

Clearly, that would not be a problem for Biden. If the Court were to declare Obamacare unconstitutional, it would only serve to make the creation of Bidencare a higher legislative priority and one that would easily be addressed as part of the efforts to address the current pandemic in a context of establishing various preventative procedures to address the future pandemics medical experts believe will arise from Global Warming.

The biggest medical issue Biden is most likely to face is the cost of ongoing medications. As we know, Trump signed 4 executive orders to cut insulin and prescription drug prices significantly. Now it will fall on Biden to carry those cuts a step further, and augment them with automatic procedures to address the next pandemic – which is unlikely to be a culling virus, and more likely to be a deadly 1918 Spanish Flu style event.

Biden will also need to address a question of undocumented or illegal immigration. He cannot fall back on the Obama-era cages and family separations which were subsequently used in the attacks on Trump.

We know that Pelosi and her California cabal are seeking to gerrymander their population to increase their representative power in Congress – without the burden of adding actual voters. They want warm bodies that bring in Federal welfare money that will offset the loss of revenue as the wealthy leave the state to avoid increases in taxes.

Biden is going to need to address the 2006 Secure Fence Act promoted by Senator Obama. The 2021 Budget has $1.35 billion for Trump's 'Wall' improvements; the steel slat wall now controls the entry of pandemic infected individuals from Mexico and will serve to halt future climate change-related pandemics.

However, Biden will still face the problem of Pelosi needing the undocumented migrants to both enhance California's political power and ability to tap the Federal coffers. Plus, Mexico has no desire to deal with unskilled, disease infected, climate migrants.

As we know from the debates, Biden approved giving illegals free healthcare that is currently denied to U.S. citizens.

Will Biden retain Obama era policies and keep the wall? Or,

will he yield to Pelosi Democrats and Reagan Republicans and see that they have an open Southern border with unrestricted access for any who enter from Mexico?

Biden will retain Trumps The United States-Mexico-Canada Agreement {USMCA}. It would be too distracting to renegotiate it, and without it, the American tax base would relocate to Mexico or Canada.

As Trump said, utilizing the practical economic effect of the trade agreement, Mexico is paying for the wall and augmenting that payment by adding heightened control of its Southern border while also tightening patrols along the U. S. Border.

As the name, "Secure Fence Act" implied, the wall is border security similar to that American NATO forces provide in Europe – using American money either through direct allocation or via the indirect freeing of assets because American funds cover those costs. And that raises the issue of national security related to the Middle East, Russia, China, North Korea, and any other geographic area or nation that might endanger America's peaceful survival.

How is Biden going to address the very real threat posed by North Korean nuclear weapons? And how is he going to address Iran? We know from the early appearance of the pandemic in Iran – before its arrival in Italy – that there must be a tight connection between it and China's Wuhan Industrial province.

We also know that China bought the loyalty of Hunter Biden and the laptop emails revealed anywhere from 10% to 50% of the proceeds went to daddy Joe, referred to as "the Chairman" who gets a cut of all the action. How will that affect controlling Iran's nuclear program which could be the basis for the next or Third World War – a Biblical Revelation timeline, which correctly identified the rise of the Nazis in 1931, has a Middle Eastern 'Apocalypse' happening in 2033. As a nuclear power with historic anger toward many other nations in the region, Iran is the likely catalyst for the war that will happen twelve-years after Biden-Harris take their oath of office.

How will the Biden-Harris administration react if and when North Korea sells its technology to Iran? And there is also the question of the Biden-Harris administration continuing to promote normalization of relations between North and South Korea.

Since Biden is "above the law' and Pelosi controls the House, we know there will be no *quid pro quo* based impeachment – even if Ukraine prosecutors decide to level Biden family-related charges against Burisma.

While Biden might be above the law, there is a question as to whether or not he will acknowledge the law. But then, if, as he once acknowledged, it might be a matter of his handlers behaving in the interest of the nation – but, Pelosi received some of the pork she wanted in the stimulus package, and the Republicans received some in the form of a return to the "Three Martini Lunch" as a means of stimulating the restaurant industry.

Average people, those who do not have "business lunches," will get some form of expanded tax or child tax credit.

Biden must get a stimulus package that devotes all its money to the people and avoids enriching special interests in California or New York City, where the movement is to encourage undocumented individuals – the new SCOTUS compliant gerrymandering – while taxing the productive rich, those building the next century source of capital growth, to the point where they leave the state.

Biden's advisors will, eventually, inform him that the only way to save New York City and Southern California will come from providing "Medicare For All" – universal healthcare for all citizens.

Biden expressed an interest in creating a vague "Bidencare" out of the "Obamacare" program which was designed to benefit big pharma. In effect, Biden declared a goal of "Repeal and Replace."

Donald Trump cut both prescription costs and co-pays – but, because of the usual time-delay issues on changes, those cuts will only really be seen after Biden takes office, and that fact will test the credibility of fact-checkers and others who refer to what promise to be substantial cuts.

Will the fact-checkers be honest, and credit Trump, or, as is often the case, be dishonest and confuse the credit in a way that praises the administration they wish to promote?

Biden will also need to focus on criminal and justice reform.

Comically, in Biden's case, this means reversing those very policies he, as a Senator, promoted and his Vice President enforced with bigoted glee.

The time has come to reverse drug prohibition on anything that is not proven to be addictive. In the case of marijuana, a plant that has been known to be beneficial since it was widely used by the Scythians era of King David, the Federal Laws must be brought into line with the decriminalization of the State level.

In the age of Covid-19, it is also important that Biden take action against tobacco, which is responsible for the annual death of twice as many Americans as Covid. Tobacco is an addictive drug and in multiple forms is responsible for various forms of cancer. With the legalization of marijuana, the tobacco industry farmers could easily switch production and the industry itself could restructure its facilities to meet the historic demand for "quality weed."

Biden also needs to ensure the nation realizes that those who seek to control the private or personal actions of others are the root of most evils in the world. This was amply demonstrated during the Prohibition Era when banning alcohol only served to remove a source of federal and state tax revenue while creating the organized crime networks that promoted violence.

We also saw the reality after Roe v Wade, when abortion once again became legal.

There is no religious justification for opposing abortion – the Bible tells us that, if a man suspects a baby is not his, his wife is to take an abortion/miscarriage inducing herbal mixture.

As presented, the "religious" position holds that, if the baby is not the husbands it will be aborted. And if those waving the Bible were really believers, they would hold, as the Scripture does, that any child conceived of a man who is not the woman's husband is to be aborted.

YES! The Bible's only mention of abortion is in support of it. But then, the context is consistent with the idea of no sex outside of marriage. Any woman who violates that rule should not be having children – hence the mandate to abort if they are not married to the father.

If we speak in terms of a "human life" then change the laws so that citizenship begins at conception and a child is a full citizen of the nation where it is conceived. At that point, where the Bible talks of human rights coming when some part of the fetus emerges from the mother, civil law would recognize it in the way many who claim to be pro-life assert it to be – from conception.

But, we must also recognize that the pro-life groups are liars who support war and military expenditures designed exclusively for the murder of foreigners. When the pro-life groups oppose foreign interventions or basing of troops on foreign soil without an explicit declaration of war mandated by the Constitution, we can say they are moral – until then, they are agents of Satan, voting on the behalf of Satan, to inflict harm on others.

Remember, when the pro-lifer overrides personal decision to forgo having a child, they might be doing so out of their desire to endanger the life of the woman or to encourage a situation where the pregnancy will result in loss of the fetus – with the emotional trauma that would impose on the woman – while also causing her to become sterile, to lose the ability to reproduce, and so the pro-life advocate is killing healthy children that woman wanted and would have had.

Pro-life is really pro-murder.

Then too, there is the matter of supporting the fetus that is being aborted because the parents cannot afford the child. Pro-life groups offer no support, no medical care during pregnancy, and they also oppose raising minimum wages to an above poverty level where people can afford to have children. Instead, they force the child on a woman and then denounce her as a "welfare queen" – because they forced her to live off the public dole.

Being the hypocrites they are, they are heard to say, "if you can't afford a child, you shouldn't have it." And they ignore the fact that the only reason the child was conceived was they denied the woman access to family planning resources or an abortion.

The beauty of the situation is, their hypocrisy carries over into almost everything that ultimately proves harmful to individuals and detrimental to society. Their agenda is "The Most Harm to the Most People" {MH2MP} through any-and-all means possible.

Biden must, if he wants an enduring legacy, ensure that

those promoting MH2MP cease to be as successful as they have been in the past.

Biden has said he sought to "restore the soul of the nation" and that, his election would "Let this grim era of demonization in America begin to end here and now." But Biden, who is himself a lawbreaker, and therefore serves the demon, has his work cut out for him. We have seen four years of demonizing Trump and have the promise legal efforts to publicize his tax returns will continue into the near future.

A fact placed in the public record on 21 December, when the House Oversight and Reform Committee panel informed the federal appeals court it would renew the quest for a subpoena for President Trump's financial records. Done properly, the panel could distract from Biden family crimes long enough to find a new distraction.

Democratic Swamp Denizens challenged Trump's victory as illegitimate and called for an end to the Electoral College. Trump has paid them back by rejecting the 2021 results as fraudulent and pushing things to expose problems on both sides of the aisle – none of which will change the outcome.

Biden's electoral victory was matched by a legitimate popular vote victory. But, as with Hillary, his majority was accounted for by Southern California – who's politicians would later be the driving force behind the impeachment and continue to harass Trump.

On 22 November, when many counties were still counting ballots, Biden had a seven-million vote lead over trump that could readily be erased by again excluding California and New York City votes.

Biden has matched Trump's 2016 electoral college victory and did it with a record 80-million votes to Trump's record 73.9-million to gain a six-million vote advantage – one-million from New York and the balance from California.

Historically, those states are the focal point of Conservative-liberal conflicts and therefore became a focal point for censorship, control over human conduct, blacklisting, and unconstitutional behavior. Without the Electoral College, this would mean these states control where the future is going.

There is also the historical fact California Democrats are not

Progressives – they are the ancient slave owners seeking new slaves in the form of the non-voter bodies called the undocumented.

The larger voting population in both California and New York City allows them to sway the popular vote in the Presidential Election – which is one of the reasons there is an Electoral College.

On Monday, 30 November 2020, a challenge to Trump's July directive to exclude illegals reached the SCOTUS. On 18 December, the justices declined to weigh in on the legality of an exclusion plan because the case "*is riddled with contingencies and speculation that impede judicial review.*" One issue is the plausibility of the Census Bureau being able to identify those to be excluded.

At stake is the loss of House seats for California, Texas, and New Jersey. The facts also rest on the meaning behind, "*the whole number of persons in each State.*" Does it mean visitors, tourists, or others who are not legal residents count? And do they count both where they are (out of state students) and where they reside?

If the Court rules they are to be counted, by extension, that would mean tourists and other transients must also be counted – if the count is "*as of/at a date certain.*" If the court rules to exclude transients, does that still allow those illegally physically in residence – even if they had illegally arrived the day before the census?

According to the Constitution {Amendment 14, section 2.1.1}, representation relies on "*counting the whole number of persons in each State, excluding Indians not taxed.*"

In theory, SCOTUS could extend that "*not taxed*" provision to include tourists, transients, and those lacking a Social Security number, which is now issued at birth or upon obtaining legal status – meaning illegals should be excluded.

There are numerous ramifications to the census issue.

Those who fall under the category of illegal would include a hostile invasion force. If the invasion occurred in a zero-year, they would be among "the whole number of persons" in the decennial census period. Then there is the non-violent issue of foreign troops transported to the USA for training – are they to be included in the census?

After all, they are legally in residence. And, if the SCOTUS ruling allows counting illegals, is not perfectly phrased, any state or community containing a military facility has the potential to legally gerrymander the population to gain representation.

Now, the answer will be part of the Biden legacy – creating a means to distort representation through a legally acceptable form of a gerrymander that then shapes the proportion of federal funds going to the guilty states to support illegals. If they are counted, they gain the fruits of representation.

The year 2020 is a transitional year. We saw the same effect in 1933 when the United States received Franklin Delano Roosevelt and Germany saw the rise of Adolph Hitler.

In 1933, Hedy Lamarr presented full-frontal nudity in the film "Ecstasy" and Prohibition was repealed. Four years later, in 1937, the same conservative forces behind Prohibition made marijuana illegal. It wasn't just the FDR administration, 1933 was a year of global choices. And the World chose to have a World War.

In the transition era defined by the election of Donald John Trump, we are again entering a conflict period where Conservatives get crushed. But Biden is a classic Swamp Denizen and therefore is not the one to fully crush them. As with Hitler and FDR, war will be necessary – World War or Pandemic War – does it matter, and will it be eight to twelve years away (2028-2032)?

Can Biden be the next FDR?

Has a mythological Satan been playing some form of a game with us? Or is there a different player controlling events?

On 30 November, SLATE published a Human Interest piece by Heather Schwedel entitled, *"Famed Christmas Witch Melania Trump Delivers Her Most Unlikely Holiday Display Yet."*

You know we will need to think about the idea that Melania is a *"Famed Christmas Witch."* We'll play with it a bit more in terms of the mystical that seems so popular that a journalist can get away with calling the First lady a *"Famed Christmas Witch"*

In the nation that gave us the Salem Witch Trials, it might be poetic justice for the cycle, to begin with, a Witch as FLOTUS. After all, it's no more ridiculous than yelling Trump is a crook, but not being able to cite a single statutory crime.

For now, let's deal with the possible issue of "Satan's Vote."

In Christian theology he's the ruler of Hell, a rebellious angle; alternatively, in the Jewish belief structure, he's an angel *"who is commanded by God to tempt humans to sin, to accuse the sinners, and to carry out God's punishment."* {Merriam-Webster dictionary} If we adopt the Jewish definition, Satan is a good guy following his boss's orders.

What definition applies, and does Satan get a vote in national elections? Does the Bible get a vote – and if so, which Bible? All of them or just the one bigots want to use to justify their suppression of their fellow humans?

It is a way of asking if there was fraud in the process.

If there were a Satan, how would he Vote – for Biden? Biden has boasted of *quid pro quo* blackmail and it does appear his son Hunter launders political bribe money for foreign nations seeking influence in Washington politics.

Did he want to tell Biden, *"It's Your Time"*?

Or is there another force at work, one that wanted to give this success to Biden as compensation for all the emotional losses in his life?

Of course, that argues all kinds of mystical forces – not unlike the pattern seen in the POTUS Cousins and 4-Sisters. It's a bit like electing a 2nd Catholic 60-years after the first – who was elected in a zero-year – then matching him to the first female vice president.

Since Satan isn't a registered voter, the votes he casts would be fraud, and it would also be fraud if he or his boss were to influence the election – meaning Trump's claim of fraud would have legitimacy among those who might believe in magical forces controlling human destiny. But only if we ignore documented *sub-rosa* history. Or view that *sub-rosa* process as proof of some divine hand manipulating history since the time of Charlemagne.

The only real difference between the 2016 and 2020 electoral outcome was that, in 2020, Democrats made an effort to squeeze a small additional margin in the high-income Red State districts they dominate, thus managing to squeak through a slim electoral victory where they had previously been crushed.

In 2016, Clinton amassed 62.5 million votes against Trump's

61.2 million – so, only a 1.3 million vote margin. But, the actions of "faithless electors," turned an Electoral College tally of 306:232, into the recorded 304:227. On 14 December Biden will receive the higher tally – again, consistent with a POTUS Cousin descended from three of the 4-Sisters.

In 2020, the significance comes from there being roughly 27 million more people involved in the process. As a result, Harris-Biden is going to need to justify their actions and decisions to a record number of involved voters. Or, MSM might distract voters and seek to blame Trump for Biden's flaws and failures.

Though, since the DJIA broke through the 30,000 barriers on 24 November, Harris-Biden will need to ensure the that record is secure and exceeded by at least as much as Trump exceeded the Obama-Biden highs.

But what of the *sub-rosa*, the confidential or hidden system that controlled all of America's elections? We've mentioned it, the idea of POTUS Cousins and the 4-Sisters descendancy.

Unlike her husband, HRC is neither a POTUS Cousin nor a descendant of the 4-Sisters. It, therefore, followed that she would lose to DJT who, while not being a POTUS Cousin, is a descendant of two of the 4-Sisters.

However, in the race between JRB and DJT, JRB is both a POTUS Cousin and a descendant of three of the 4-Sisters – and that keeps American history intact. As for the zero-year curse, since, as with HRC, his vice president meets neither kinship standard, she is unlikely to replace JRB – unless Satan's Vote supports the Death of America slogan which, since 1979, has been the Iranian Revolution anti-American Shia political slogan and, since August 2020, it has also been the slogan associated with Antifa/BLM rioters in both New York City and California.

On 22 August, actor James Woods observed: *"New Democrat logo spells out 'Death to America' The new DNC logo, meanwhile, which claims to say 'D20' (as in Democrats '20) places a map of the United States inside the zero, appearing to read 'D 2 America' or 'Death to America.'"*

While there are negative forces at work, in a transition year, it serves us well to look at changes or positive aspects of the Trump administration that Biden will need to improve upon.

In 2019, carbon emissions fell by 9%, and then the pandemic drove them down further – improving air quality while reducing the American contribution to climate gases causing Global Warming.

Will Harris-Biden continue to improve American air quality while also growing the economy? And will they find a way to put to rest the election interference propaganda that was the Democratic *"Russia, Russia, Russia"* nonsense, which Trump flipped to allege election fraud or manipulation on the part of Democrats or some foreign actor?

The Democrats spent four years indoctrinating the public to believe the elections were dishonest and that the Electoral College should be dropped and national elections decided by popular vote – so California and New York can take control of the outcome to the detriment of the rest of the nation.

On 22 November, Trump Tweeted a curious assertion that only historians could prove true because the current population is not interested in facts: *"In certain swing states, there were more votes than people who voted, and in big numbers. Does that not really matter? Stopping Poll Watchers, voting for unsuspecting people, fake ballots and so much more. Such egregious conduct. We will win!"*

That said, while Trump's people were still trying to ensure they had all the dotted-I-cross-T legal nonsense had run its course, Biden was granted the slogan website "BuildBackBetter.gov" as part of the acknowledgment by Emily Murphy, the administrator of the General Services Administration, he was the presumptive President-elect. This was accompanied by the release, on 23 November, of the initial senior staff picks for his administration.

As expected, there were numerous attacks on Trump by those seeking to be in the good graces of the new President, and there were even assertions of continued investigations into Trump's Tax Returns.

The investigations are a good move. They will allow MSM to focus on something other than Biden and thus provide him ample cover during the first hundred days when the media is usually dissecting a new administration. And, of course, if all else fails, we have the mysticism.

From the 4-Sisters link to the Christmas Witch, we can say that mystic elements abound. And the idea Melania of associating with being a "witch" introduces the possibility that she could be a seer who is endowed with spiritual insight or knowledge has been revealed in the White House Christmas decor.

Let's consider the assertions Heather Schwedel made in her SLATE article and compare them to what we know occurred in the Trump administration; then project into Biden's time.

Schwedel bemoaned the fact "This could have been her best haunted Christmas yet: In a lame-duck holiday season," if not for the normality which defined the 2020 decorative theme. So let's consider the normality in terms of the possibility that the decorative schemes foretold that which was to come. In that context, Covid-19 might well have been predicted in 2017 as a state of being that would begin in December 2019 or, maybe, 2020.

In describing 2017, Schwedel tells us, *"That first year, she took my breath away with the hallway full of vases holding bouquets of skeletal dead branches, lit from below so they projected nightmarish shadows on the ceilings."*

In 2019, Christmas in China was marked by the government hiding the emergence of Covid-19. The shadows of an emerging pandemic were reported by the Taiwanese, but when The World Health Organization queried China, their response was to downplay its significance.

Still, the *skeletal dead branches* of the virus could be seen as the elderly who were culled or cut from their living ancestral tree. The vases would then become their resting places – today, over 52-percent of Chinese dead are cremated.

On 30 January, the British newspaper, THE SUN, published: *"TORCHING EVIDENCE China is cremating bodies in secret to hide true extent of death toll, says new report."* Is that yet another nightmarish shadow on the ceiling?

If not, consider a CD Report issued on 30 November in which it was stated they now have hard evidence that Covid-19 was in Washington, Oregon, and California between 13 and 16

December 2019. There were also antibodies discovered in blood donation samples collected between 30 December 2019 and 17 January 2020 in Connecticut, Massachusetts, Rhode Island, Iowa, and Michigan.

The researchers noted that "*These findings also highlight the value of blood donations as a source for conducting SARS-CoV-2 surveillance.*" The research also affirmed earlier research published in JAMA Internal Medicine indicating that no more than 23 percent of the U.S. has antibodies for the virus.

Schwedel mentions 2018 was marked by "*red trees. Surely you remember them: the blood-colored cones that looked like they had been plucked out of a coniferous forest for muppets in hell itself. They were chilling.*"

Red trees, the color of leaves in the fall associated with Kousa dogwood (Cornus kousa), a deciduous tree native to China, shedding trees are native to many regions of the world and are quite common in the North Eastern Corridor of the United States, where most of the Covid-19 deaths initially occurred.

Red is associated with Communism and the War Horseman of the Apocalypse. In 2020, China was reported to be engaged in several minor military actions. But at its heart, Red is an emotional color of great intensity and is associated with fire, fury, love, and passion – can we deny that those traits defined the 2020 election cycle?

Then we have Schwedel's view on the 2019 theme: "*when a series of star sculptures that resembled glass shards were hung from the ceiling of another hallway, and, what's more, the first lady herself appeared in a video placing tiny wreaths in the windows of a dollhouse-sized White House in a display that could only summon an image of torturing tiny voodoo dolls.*"

It would seem that lends itself to several interpretations, but why move past "*an image of torturing tiny voodoo dolls*"?

What magic, witchcraft, or voodoo, shall we see unfold in 2021? Biden is inaugurated, the zero-year curse sees an attack on his life – we need no assassin, we have Covid-19 or whatever caused his twin brain aneurysms. No matter, Kamala isn't a POTUS Cousin and has, as yet, no known kinship to the 4-Sisters, so Biden cannot die or even be sufficiently impaired to cease performing his duties.

Then we have the post-election 2020 display: *"a stunningly generic Christmas scene out of a commercial for Michael's, complete with ornaments, holly, red bows, and a miniature train. Just colossally uninspired. Other years' décor showed us that this is a woman capable of true darkness, that inside her soul thrives a garden of evil blazing shrubbery, so I really just can't with the pretty lights and appropriate color schemes."*

WOW! The FLOTUS scene set before the Electoral College votes to formally make Biden the President-elect is *"stunningly generic"* and lacks the Satanic darkness of spirit which Schwedel saw in earlier years.

But does that mean the year 2022 will be generic? And what does it mean for a year to have a generic quality?

The United States has seen nineteen years of generic military conflict. To some extent, President Trump has worked to unwind and un-entangle American forces from the generic and murderous rampage begun by George W. Bush.

We can say Bush's 19-year conflict "generic" because it is not associated with a clearly defined enemy or a formal, Constitutionally defined, Declaration of War. Since World War Two, all U.S. military actions have fallen into a generic category – no governmental enemy or entity internationally recognized to enter into a peace treaty has been attacked.

What generic war can we expect in 2022? And will it be initiated before or after the mid-term election – yet another issue to challenge POTUS-46.

Could FLOTUS Trump be a witch? Or is she a sage?

Has her decoration foretold the pandemic that would emerge in China, its dead branches in "crematory vases" symbolizing family branches that were to be culled by Covid-19 in 2020?

With the vases lining the halls of America's White House, did she foresee the dead branches of American families?

Covid-19 is real, it is with us, and, like so many other threats to the health of individuals, it will remain with us. The challenge for President Biden shall be seeing that no new virus or plague befalls the nation.

With the Covid-19 pandemic, the nation has learned the true importance of stimulus packages, Universal Healthcare, and maybe this will translate into understanding other items of importance.

There is the challenge of Student Loan Debt which needs to be reduced or eliminated. If Biden simply exercises his executive powers, he can cancel the debt – but that would take income assets off the books and make his economy look bad.

Were he to allow the debt to be documented to the IRS and act as a tax-related credit, the government would still be writing the money off, but in a way that rewards earnings and provides cashflow which would go directly to building the GDP and taxable income of those companies whose goods or services are being bought.

Curiously, in this way, writing off the Student Loans rewards those who work. Those who do not work, who do not generate and pay taxes on earned income, will still be required to pay a portion of their student loans annually.

Granted, it's not easily grasped – effectively every tax dollar paid is matched by a write-off of the annual Student Debt payment. If the loan payment is $200 per month or $2,400 per year, and you pay $2,400 in taxes, $2,400 of your loan will be deemed paid.

Pay $10,000 in income taxes and your student loan balance will be credited for $10,000. The higher your earned income tax liability, the faster your student loan will vanish. But slack-off and fail to earn a taxable income, you are going to need to still pay the Student Loan plus accrued interest.

While there are calls to cancel Student Loan payments, doing so cheats those who have already paid their loans or paid cash for their education. And simply canceling loans that are currently on the books has the effect of cheating those who will be first entering college or university in the years to come. It cheats the student who graduates High School in 2021 or thereafter. It also cheats those individuals who are first finishing their undergraduate work and are about to embark on the next phase towards a Masters or Doctorate.

An executive order can erase a current taxpayer liability, and so erase a government financial asset (account receivable), but it does nothing for those who carry no debt or have yet to graduate.

The Challenge to President Biden is to get Congress to create a structure that rewards education – and effectively makes it free for those who complete their studies and put their learning to work.

Done properly, since education is effectively free, schools will not need to offer conventional scholarships. Instead, that money could go to enriching the student's academic experience – it could provide resources for specialized in-depth study or experience.

The Greek philosopher Diogenes stated: *"The foundation of every state is the education of its youth."* America cannot afford to have the cost of education undermine its foundation.

CHAPTER SEVEN – Deadly Numbers 2019
"Oderint dum metuant,
Let them hate me, as long as they fear me."
~ Suetonius

At this stage in the Trump Card series, it is well worth the space to present the death numbers related to the Chart in Chapter 1 and the Covid-19 pandemic.

The CDC posts weekly death numbers, which are presented here in charts showing five weeks per page. It should be noted that, as of this writing, the CDC has yet to post the actual death total for 2019, so the number is derived from provided weekly data.

A CDC 2 December posting states:

"As of December 1, 2020, an average of around 952 people per day have died from COVID-19 in the U.S. since the first case was confirmed in the country on January 20th. On an average day, nearly 8,000 people die from all causes in the United States, based on data from 2019. Based on the latest information, one in nine deaths each day can be attributed to COVID-19 since January 20th. The daily death toll from seasonal flu, using preliminary maximum estimates from the 2019-2020 influenza season, stood at an average of almost 332 people."

Average deaths compared to a weekly data total (2,852,609) and yields a mortality rate of about 0.87 – the same rate derived for 2017 and 2018. Assuming this reflects the Baby-Boomers reaching their 74-year life expectancy, it follows that the normal total deaths for 2020 and, possibly, the next decade, will be in that same range or, due to pre-1958 birthrate of 24 per 1000 people, the next decade could see a ten-percent higher death rate. Because the 2020 rate is below 12 per thousand, and when we consider that, in 1958, there were 20 million children under the age of 4, and those who are still alive would be age 62 or older, the effect will be dramatic.

Given a pre-census estimated population of 331 million and, as Boomer's die, an anticipated one percent annual decline, about 3.3 deaths are expected. Week 50 of 2020, 3 million were recorded in the CDC weekly mortality data. This means, Covid-19 has failed to increase the age adjusted anticipated deaths – hence, it is a virus culling those who would have died within a year.

Over the last three years (2017-2019), the average death rate has gradually increased and the birth rate has declined. Based on those three years, where the first of the Baby-Boomers were below the expected life expectancy, a death rate of 0.87 appears to be the average. Male Boomers have reached their 76-year life expectancy and will begin to die faster. Even without Covid-19, death rates will increase.

We should note, on 3 December, it was reported that, based on CDC data, *"Joe Biden predicted another 250,000 deaths from COVID-19 by the end of the year."*

While it seems dramatic, as the following chart shows, what Biden said approximates the 2019 deaths from all causes and can be seen as is ridiculous in terms of Covid-19.

CDC Dr. Robert Redfield said, *"The reality is that December and January and February are going to be rough times. I actually believe they are going to be the most difficult time in the public health history of this nation."*

Biden, the man who will become POTUS on 20 January, is asserting Covid-19 alone would cause about 8.9 thousand deaths a day while the CDC website states: *"On an average day, nearly 8,000 people die from all causes."*

Has the CDC informed Biden of something other than what they *"published by John Elflein, Dec 2, 2020"*? Or, has Biden once again screwed up the numerical data and illogically exaggerated it?

Clearly, Biden's assertion is illogical, he is saying as many people will die in six weeks as have died since the first reported case in February. Moreover, the weekly statistics show that the deaths are actually from multiple causes with Covid-19 as the underlying trigger that accelerates the death.

The same news report citing Biden's recorded statement has this to say: *"According to a project from Johns Hopkins University, the United States remains the country with the highest number of coronavirus cases in the world: 13,881,620. 1,488,992 people have died in the United States since the start of the pandemic, and 41,268,029 people have been cured."*

United States Deaths in 2019			United States Deaths in 2020		
All Causes		Natural	All Causes		Natural
291,654		268,331	298,132		273,695
291,676		267,920	295,863		270,946
284,384		260,763	331,969		307,493
269,776		246,388	350,797		324,945
265,209		240,515	295,673		267,948
235,058		180,283	306,767		278,670
232,057		177,506	312,863		286,305
236,275		180,058	288,422		265,763
247,395		188,059	288,050		270,978
261,498	Average	223,314	307,615	Average	282,971
Comparing first 45 weeks of 2019 and 2020					
46,117	All	{2020 less 2019}		Natural	59,658

However, a look at "Worldmeter" – which gets its data from John Hopkins and other sources – states that globally, there have been 65,290,620 Coronavirus cases and 1,507,570 deaths.

So, is this nonsense about "*1,488,992 people have died in the United States since the start of the pandemic*" a deliberate Biden lie or evidence that he cannot read, recall, or understand factual data?

The numbers being cited are globally, and directly related to events in the United States. But this wording and reporting might be symptomatic of the quality of comments and media we can expect to define the Harris-Biden administration.

Comparing both averages – deaths from "All Causes" and those from "Natural Causes" – for the first 45 weeks of 2019 and 2020, we see our magical 46k is again present. We also see, a "Natural" death average higher than the "All Causes" increase.

Since "All causes" includes accidents and Covid-19, Covid may have saved lives – an average of 13,541 per 5-week interval – we can attribute that to younger workers staying home. Remember, Covid targets for death those over 55 – the Baby-Boomers – and mostly those over 65.

We might also note the reason why this is a "culling virus" – it kills Baby-Boomers and Silent Generation members whose medical conditions would have them die soon. Both Biden and Trump are members of this group – Trump is healthy, Biden is sickly.

At first, that inference might seem callous. But, it is rational to consider that the first Baby-Boomers are seventy-five years-old and within two years of *"mortality age,"* and a War Baby, *"a person born in 1941 [had] a life expectancy of 62.81."* Those who exceeded 63 are both among the current statistics and the reason the Social Security program is said to be out of money – they weren't expected to collect on what was a *German designed 1870 Ponzi Scheme.*

It should be noted that a similar Ponzi Scheme pattern or basic concept was repeated in the drafting of the Paris Climate Accord.

With the climate accord, the industrialized nations guilty of the most pollution are free to outsource pollution generating processes to non-signatory nations. There is also the fact that the date is, as Greta Thunberg has repeatedly pointed out, far too far into the future.

If national leaders were honestly interested in reducing their pollution they would be instituting transition programs like that in China – where all vehicles sold after 2025 will be electric.

******

The next eleven pages provide death data for 2019 – in five week groups. Chapter 08 will provide the same charts for 2020 – with the data available at the time of this book's publication.

CENTER FOR DISEASE CONTROL & PREVENTION weekly data https://www.cdc.gov/						
Jurisdiction of Occurrence	United States					
MMWR Year	2019					
MMWR Week	1	2	3	4	5	
Week Ending Date	01/15/19	01/22/19	01/29/19	02/05/19	02/12/19	
All Cause	58,474	58,514	58,354	58,034	58,278	
Natural Cause	53,581	53,760	53,807	53,525	53,658	
Septicemia (A40-A41)	788	820	807	829	793	4,037
Malignant neoplasms (C00-C97)	11,655	11,886	11,878	11,731	11,752	58,902
Diabetes mellitus (E10-E14)	1,941	1,758	1,826	1,926	1,901	9,352
Alzheimer disease (G30)	2,413	2,451	2,609	2,447	2,520	12,440
Influenza and pneumonia (J09-J18)	1,272	1,319	1,331	1,241	1,313	6,476
Chronic lower respiratory diseases (J40-J47)	3,459	3,616	3,388	3,444	3,390	17,297
Other diseases of respiratory system	911	937	956	918	923	4,645
Nephritis, nephrotic syndrome and nephrosis	1,089	1,035	1,112	1,054	1,076	5,366
Symptoms, signs and abnormal clinical and laboratory findings, not elsewhere classified	651	599	596	643	596	3,085
Diseases of heart (I00-I09,I11,I13,I20-I51)	13,896	13,645	13,639	13,755	13,777	68,712
Cerebrovascular diseases (I60-I69)	2,888	3,095	3,112	2,985	3,105	15,185
COVID-19 (U071, Multiple Cause of Death)	0	0	0	0	0	0
COVID-19 (U071, Underlying Cause of Death)	0	0	0	0	0	0

	United States 2019					
MMWR Week	6	7	8	9	10	
Week Ending Date	02/19/19	02/26/19	03/05/19	03/12/19	03/19/19	
All Cause	58,663	58,120	58,135	58,074	58,684	
Natural Cause	53,743	53,512	53,565	53,275	53,825	
Septicemia (A40-A41)	820	817	826	803	800	4,066
Malignant neoplasms (C00-C97)	11,716	11,687	11,779	11,548	11,840	58,570
Diabetes mellitus (E10-E14)	1,823	1,901	1,823	1,893	1,810	9,250
Alzheimer disease (G30)	2,580	2,558	2,516	2,373	2,461	12,488
Influenza and pneumonia (J09-J18)	1,338	1,407	1,412	1,429	1,476	7,062
Chronic lower respiratory diseases (J40-J47)	3,515	3,423	3,497	3,433	3,443	17,311
Other diseases of respiratory system	946	926	937	862	942	4,613
Nephritis, nephrotic syndrome and nephrosis	1,041	1,089	1,093	1,018	1,043	5,284
Symptoms, signs and abnormal clinical and laboratory findings, not elsewhere classified	625	632	591	609	627	3,084
Diseases of heart (I00-I09,I11,I13,I20-I51)	13,671	13,754	13,562	13,916	13,833	68,736
Cerebrovascular diseases (I60-I69)	2,990	3,002	3,058	3,005	3,119	15,174
COVID-19 (U071, Multiple Cause of Death)	0	0	0	0	0	0
COVID-19 (U071, Underlying Cause of Death)	0	0	0	0	0	0

	United States					
	2019					
MMWR Week	11	12	13	14	15	
Week Ending Date	03/26/19	04/02/19	04/09/19	04/16/19	04/23/19	
All Cause	58,023	57,220	56,776	56,729	55,636	
Natural Cause	53,421	52,535	52,129	51,879	50,799	
Septicemia (A40-A41)	820	776	835	776	778	3,985
Malignant neoplasms (C00-C97)	11,746	11,528	11,450	11,468	11,323	57,515
Diabetes mellitus (E10-E14)	1,748	1,814	1,787	1,740	1,760	8,849
Alzheimer disease (G30)	2,467	2,390	2,457	2,440	2,245	11,999
Influenza and pneumonia (J09-J18)	1,487	1,421	1,318	1,224	1,118	6,568
Chronic lower respiratory diseases (J40-J47)	3,479	3,384	3,402	3,344	3,345	16,954
Other diseases of respiratory system	942	929	918	832	899	4,520
Nephritis, nephrotic syndrome and nephrosis	1,109	1,077	996	1,021	998	5,201
Symptoms, signs and abnormal clinical and laboratory findings, not elsewhere classified	621	567	619	610	627	3,044
Diseases of heart (I00-I09,I11,I13,I20-I51)	13,572	13,440	13,274	13,258	12,806	66,350
Cerebrovascular diseases (I60-I69)	3,069	2,985	3,048	2,994	2,969	15,065
COVID-19 (U071, Multiple Cause of Death)	0	0	0	0	0	0
COVID-19 (U071, Underlying Cause of Death)	0	0	0	0	0	0

	United States 2019					
MMWR Week	16	17	18	19	20	
Week Ending Date	04/30/19	05/07/19	05/14/19	05/21/19	05/28/19	
All Cause	54,590	53,770	54,118	53,602	53,696	
Natural Cause	50,047	49,146	49,358	48,811	49,026	
Septicemia (A40-A41)	768	733	729	730	679	3,639
Malignant neoplasms (C00-C97)	11,260	11,202	11,347	11,362	11,529	56,700
Diabetes mellitus (E10-E14)	1,660	1,712	1,669	1,681	1,646	8,368
Alzheimer disease (G30)	2,282	2,247	2,210	2,151	2,209	11,099
Influenza and pneumonia (J09-J18)	1,038	1,007	940	866	836	4,687
Chronic lower respiratory diseases (J40-J47)	3,221	3,095	3,017	3,121	2,979	15,433
Other diseases of respiratory system	846	868	880	828	814	4,236
Nephritis, nephrotic syndrome and nephrosis	1,012	976	996	956	965	4,905
Symptoms, signs and abnormal clinical and laboratory findings, not elsewhere classified	588	567	571	580	627	2,933
Diseases of heart (I00-I09,I11,I13,I20-I51)	12,974	12,583	12,549	12,377	12,523	63,006
Cerebrovascular diseases (I60-I69)	2,854	2,815	2,917	2,783	2,770	14,139
COVID-19 (U071, Multiple Cause of Death)	0	0	0	0	0	0
COVID-19 (U071, Underlying Cause of Death)	0	0	0	0	0	0

MMWR Week	United States 2019					
	21	22	23	24	25	
Week Ending Date	06/04/19	06/11/19	06/18/19	06/25/19	07/02/19	
All Cause	53,829	52,858	53,305	52,793	52,424	
Natural Cause	49,018	47,856	48,099	47,978	47,564	
Septicemia (A40-A41)	672	684	686	677	656	3,375
Malignant neoplasms (C00-C97)	11,656	11,301	11,225	11,489	11,344	57,015
Diabetes mellitus (E10-E14)	1,637	1,514	1,684	1,625	1,569	8,029
Alzheimer disease (G30)	2,204	2,226	2,245	2,230	2,143	11,048
Influenza and pneumonia (J09-J18)	806	816	808	758	759	3,947
Chronic lower respiratory diseases (J40-J47)	3,052	2,978	2,975	2,913	2,801	14,719
Other diseases of respiratory system	792	818	801	833	775	4,019
Nephritis, nephrotic syndrome and nephrosis	901	968	926	988	984	4,767
Symptoms, signs and abnormal clinical and laboratory findings, not elsewhere classified	606	520	582	584	553	2,845
Diseases of heart (I00-I09,I11,I13,I20-I51)	12,498	12,217	12,175	12,078	12,022	60,990
Cerebrovascular diseases (I60-I69)	2,708	2,743	2,728	2,593	2,774	13,546
COVID-19 (U071, Multiple Cause of Death)	0	0	0	0	0	0
COVID-19 (U071, Underlying Cause of Death)	0	0	0	0	0	0

	United States					
	2019					
MMWR Week	26	27	28	29	30	
Week Ending Date	07/09/19	07/16/19	07/23/19	07/30/19	08/06/19	
All Cause	52,325	52,505	52,078	51,796	51,815	
Natural Cause	47,378	47,135	47,025	46,781	46,739	
Septicemia (A40-A41)	680	694	696	657	695	3,422
Malignant neoplasms (C00-C97)	11,433	11,201	11,374	11,310	11,391	56,709
Diabetes mellitus (E10-E14)	1,556	1,585	1,533	1,636	1,537	7,847
Alzheimer disease (G30)	2,111	2,154	2,124	2,099	2,147	10,635
Influenza and pneumonia (J09-J18)	768	732	688	691	700	3,579
Chronic lower respiratory diseases (J40-J47)	2,802	2,766	2,798	2,704	2,609	13,679
Other diseases of respiratory system	786	771	736	747	789	3,829
Nephritis, nephrotic syndrome and nephrosis	901	868	992	930	927	4,618
Symptoms, signs and abnormal clinical and laboratory findings, not elsewhere classified	610	599	600	612	572	2,993
Diseases of heart (I00-I09,I11,I13,I20-I51)	12,064	12,184	11,882	11,687	11,767	59,584
Cerebrovascular diseases (I60-I69)	2,688	2,705	2,691	2,652	2,652	13,388
COVID-19 (U071, Multiple Cause of Death)	0	0	0	0	0	0
COVID-19 (U071, Underlying Cause of Death)	0	0	0	0	0	0

	United States 2019					
MMWR Week	31	32	33	34	35	
Week Ending Date	08/13/19	08/20/19	08/27/19	09/03/19	09/10/19	
All Cause	51,558	51,856	51,132	51,149	51,296	
Natural Cause	46,636	46,715	46,173	46,155	46,378	
Septicemia (A40-A41)	683	634	631	654	678	3,280
Malignant neoplasms (C00-C97)	11,433	11,344	11,352	11,441	11,432	57,002
Diabetes mellitus (E10-E14)	1,509	1,562	1,496	1,488	1,457	7,512
Alzheimer disease (G30)	2,149	2,121	2,066	2,162	2,131	10,629
Influenza and pneumonia (J09-J18)	723	691	674	649	692	3,429
Chronic lower respiratory diseases (J40-J47)	2,592	2,612	2,545	2,619	2,521	12,889
Other diseases of respiratory system	811	789	758	695	727	3,780
Nephritis, nephrotic syndrome and nephrosis	893	910	930	870	844	4,447
Symptoms, signs and abnormal clinical and laboratory findings, not elsewhere classified	582	636	597	539	583	2,937
Diseases of heart (I00-I09,I11,I13,I20-I51)	11,842	11,641	11,606	11,513	11,593	58,195
Cerebrovascular diseases (I60-I69)	2,656	2,649	2,693	2,679	2,729	13,406
COVID-19 (U071, Multiple Cause of Death)	0	0	0	0	0	0
COVID-19 (U071, Underlying Cause of Death)	0	0	0	0	0	0

	United States 2019					
MMWR Week	36	37	38	39	40	
Week Ending Date	09/17/19	09/24/19	10/01/19	10/08/19	10/15/19	
All Cause	51,959	51,759	51,910	52,875	52,684	
Natural Cause	46,714	46,868	47,085	47,981	47,627	
Septicemia (A40-A41)	661	713	646	752	671	3,443
Malignant neoplasms (C00-C97)	11,399	11,422	11,300	11,694	11,470	57,285
Diabetes mellitus (E10-E14)	1,441	1,547	1,544	1,601	1,591	7,724
Alzheimer disease (G30)	2,178	2,174	2,193	2,183	2,305	11,033
Influenza and pneumonia (J09-J18)	677	639	695	707	660	3,378
Chronic lower respiratory diseases (J40-J47)	2,573	2,660	2,601	2,669	2,628	13,131
Other diseases of respiratory system	769	730	802	803	858	3,962
Nephritis, nephrotic syndrome and nephrosis	926	854	927	942	955	4,604
Symptoms, signs and abnormal clinical and laboratory findings, not elsewhere classified	601	551	573	641	623	2,989
Diseases of heart (I00-I09,I11,I13,I20-I51)	11,709	11,742	11,743	11,798	11,766	58,758
Cerebrovascular diseases (I60-I69)	2,645	2,807	2,673	2,846	2,780	13,751
COVID-19 (U071, Multiple Cause of Death)	0	0	0	0	0	0
COVID-19 (U071, Underlying Cause of Death)	0	0	0	0	0	0

	United States 2019					
MMWR Week	41	42	43	44	45	
Week Ending Date	10/22/19	10/29/19	11/05/19	11/12/19	11/19/19	
All Cause	53,220	54,440	54,156	54,214	55,802	
Natural Cause	48,282	49,563	49,424	49,292	50,834	
Septicemia (A40-A41)	752	723	725	726	787	3,713
Malignant neoplasms (C00-C97)	11,646	11,701	11,659	11,610	11,822	58,438
Diabetes mellitus (E10-E14)	1,539	1,627	1,617	1,665	1,690	8,138
Alzheimer disease (G30)	2,309	2,347	2,406	2,325	2,442	11,829
Influenza and pneumonia (J09-J18)	724	771	763	782	813	3,853
Chronic lower respiratory diseases (J40-J47)	2,654	2,758	2,702	2,826	2,721	13,661
Other diseases of respiratory system	805	831	811	844	879	4,170
Nephritis, nephrotic syndrome and nephrosis	946	971	993	970	1,060	4,940
Symptoms, signs and abnormal clinical and laboratory findings, not elsewhere classified	629	635	604	607	662	3,137
Diseases of heart (I00-I09,I11,I13,I20-I51)	11,916	12,527	12,410	12,111	12,664	61,628
Cerebrovascular diseases (I60-I69)	2,820	2,866	2,960	2,946	2,960	14,552
COVID-19 (U071, Multiple Cause of Death)	0	0	0	0	0	0
COVID-19 (U071, Underlying Cause of Death)	0	0	0	0	0	0

	United States					
	2019					
MMWR Week	46	47	48	49	50	
Week Ending Date	11/26/19	12/03/19	12/10/19	12/17/19	12/24/19	
All Cause	56,036	56,333	55,601	57,417	57,776	
Natural Cause	51,207	51,482	50,785	52,445	52,821	
Septicemia (A40-A41)	742	727	715	815	799	3,798
Malignant neoplasms (C00-C97)	11,656	11,655	11,339	11,463	11,582	57,695
Diabetes mellitus (E10-E14)	1,731	1,710	1,735	1,842	1,789	8,807
Alzheimer disease (G30)	2,498	2,494	2,542	2,577	2,658	12,769
Influenza and pneumonia (J09-J18)	868	807	824	988	1,017	4,504
Chronic lower respiratory diseases (J40-J47)	2,830	2,937	2,885	3,125	3,129	14,906
Other diseases of respiratory system	851	887	903	840	899	4,380
Nephritis, nephrotic syndrome and nephrosis	1,038	1,025	1,029	1,034	1,075	5,201
Symptoms, signs and abnormal clinical and laboratory findings, not elsewhere classified	645	663	663	638	691	3,300
Diseases of heart (I00-I09,I11,I13,I20-I51)	12,939	12,992	12,990	13,557	13,174	65,652
Cerebrovascular diseases (I60-I69)	2,989	3,185	3,016	3,083	3,108	15,381
COVID-19 (U071, Multiple Cause of Death)	0	0	0	0	0	0
COVID-19 (U071, Underlying Cause of Death)	0	0	0	0	0	0

	United States 2019			No Covid Dead	
MMWR Week		52			
Week Ending Date	12/31/19	01/07/20		Non-Natural Deaths	252,744
All Cause	57,581	58,637			
Natural Cause	52,760	53,663			
Septicemia (A40-A41)	763	866		Chart 1 chart	1,629
Malignant neoplasms (C00-C97)	11,667	11,495		anticipated 2,717,775	23,162
Diabetes mellitus (E10-E14)	1,784	1,899		deaths; the CDC	3,683
Alzheimer disease (G30)	2,595	2,577		December 2020	5,172
Influenza and pneumonia (J09-J18)	1,050	1,120		number in this data is	2,170
Chronic lower respiratory diseases (J40-J47)	3,265	3,353		2,852,609. This is	6,618
Other diseases of respiratory system	910	952		consistent with the	1,862
Nephritis, nephrotic syndrome and nephrosis	1,062	1,059		2017 & 2018 totals; it is	2,121
Symptoms, signs and abnormal clinical and laboratory findings, not elsewhere classified	747	758		also consistent with	1,505
Diseases of heart (I00-I09,I11,I13,I20-I51)		13,831		TOTAL DEATHS	27,089
Cerebrovascular diseases (I60-I69)	3,187	3,087		2,852,609	6,274
COVID-19 (U071, Multiple Cause of Death)	0	0			0
COVID-19 (U071, Underlying Cause of Death)	0	0			0

CHAPTER EIGHT – Daily Numbers 2020

***"A Ponzi scheme is a form of fraud that lures investors and pays profits to earlier investors with funds from more recent investors." ~* Wikipedia definition**

We concluded the previous with the German Ponzi Scheme introduced by Otto Von Bismarck to placate German Progressives of his era. In reality, because the average German died by 50, setting the retirement age at 65 ensured that the vast majority who paid in would never collect. Thus it was a tax people happily paid in expectation of beating the odds – effectively placing a bet that they would be the exception and live to win the retirement lottery.

FDR introduced the Progressive German-American concept of Social Security as a post-Great Depression program for similar Ponzi Scheme reasons and objectives.

During the Depression people had experienced bread lines and Hoovervilles; the average person knew what it was like to lack economic security and, therefore, were happy to exercise a variation on the line used by the 1931 Popeye cartoon character Wimpy: *"I'd Gladly Pay You Tuesday For A Hamburger Today."*

With Social Security, it becomes: "I'd Gladly Pay You Today for a Living Income Tomorrow." Only, as we have seen post-Carter, the promised income ceased to be one people could live on. Where the nation to adopt a Universal Basic Income (UBI) that was fixed at 150% of poverty and, funded by a 6% tax on all earned income – replacing Social Security and Welfare – everyone would prosper.

However, we are dealing with "Satan's Vote," and that means helping others is off the table. We introduced religion as the mystic genie in the bottle where pray corresponds to wishes and we forgot the admonition *"be careful what you wish for, you might get it."*

The Right-wing "prayed" and others "wished" for a solution to the PONZI SCHEME that did not involve economic intelligence. They wished Social Security would be on a sound economic footing and now, the culling virus will achieve that.

When it comes to fulfilling prayers, Satan and his Boss have a sense of humor. Rather than increase resources, they eliminated the recipients. They sent Covid-19 to kill Social Security recipients

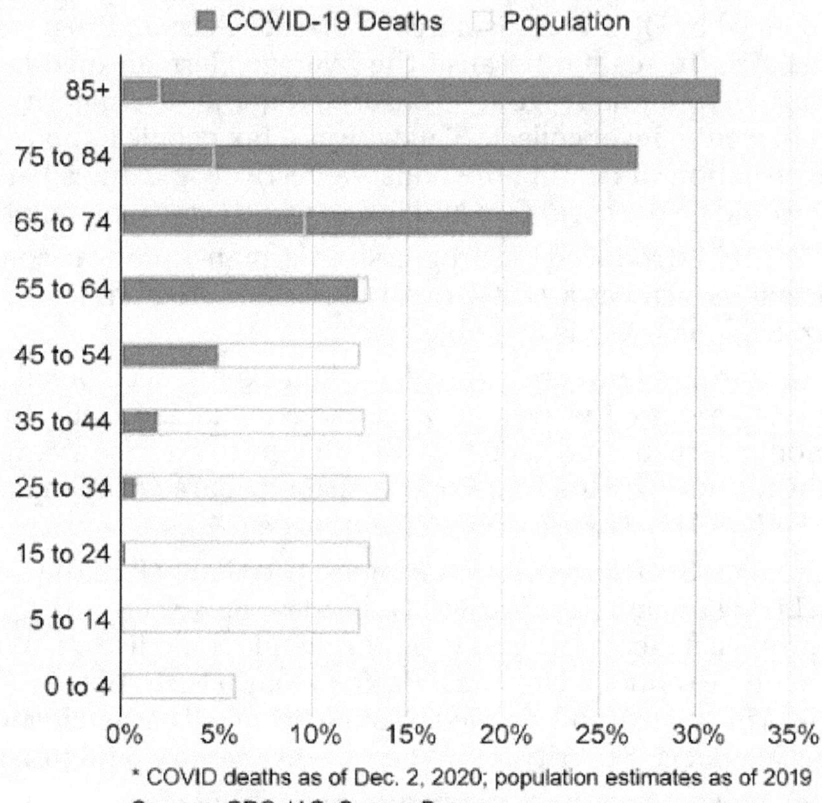

and thus we see America, the SSI nation, has the most deaths.

We have the 2020 CDC documented weekly deaths and who are most affected, and a Newsweek chart of the age ranges of those who have died shows the percentage of deaths overlaid on the group percent of the overall population.

It should be clear that the Baby-Boom generation {those in 2020 were under 76} accounts for the majority of the deaths. The

Silent Generation, those over 75, is about 60-percent of the total.

In round numbers, over 95-percent of the Covid-19 victims are over the age of 55 – the vast majority are eligible for some level of Social Security benefit. As Progressives have pointed out, those who are younger are largely composed of the poor Black and Latino minorities and, per CDC, are three times as likely to die from Covid.

Apparently: "*39.8% of all the actual welfare recipients are Black, and 38.8% of all the welfare recipients are white... Hispanic: 15.7% ... Asian: 2.4% ... Other: 3.3%*".

We need to consider the fact that welfare is received by about 19-percent of Americans. In economic terms, it would be cheaper to do away with the welfare system and install a UBI which would eliminate bureaucratic costs and ensure money only went to those here legally – those with valid Social Security numbers in a world where having the number symbolized a commitment of the nation to care for its own.

Paying for the system is easy. Bernie Sanders has asserted the simple solution – either to ensure the economic security of the current system or provided for a UBI – to eliminate the current cap on incoome subject to contribution. Do that, and Social Security would be supported by 6-12% of all personal income.

In effect, it would also tax the elite one-percent in a way that is beneficial to all and eludes forms of tax-gimmick manipulation.

To fulfill the wishes of the elite who attack Social security, the mystical entities decided to simply kill off everyone collecting Social Security or imposing medical costs on the related Medicare system.

A UBI is a Stimulus Package that is always in place and can be budgeted as an emergency fallback. It eliminates the need for a non-employment related unemployment insurance – employers might decide to offer a severance income package, or it might be part of union-negotiated packages. The cost can be covered by some form of employer purchased private insurance.

The critical reality is that a UBI allows people to purchase the basics they need to live. As a result, it doesn't really impose any cost on the economy. The 7-10 economic multiplier would be in place, and it would become more reliable for essential businesses like food, rent, utilities, and basic transportation.

It would not discourage work. Though it could encourage the arts and creative processes of the type that created the computer revolution and modern media.

Those who do not *"get it,"* should binge-watch STAR TREK. Where is the money? We hear about *"credits"*, but it is only alien societies like the Ferengi – who use Gold-Pressed Latinum currency – who have any need to "work." For members of the Federation, it would appear that everything is free and people work for the love of their endeavors.

But, that's fantasy. But it is a fantasy that could become part of our daily reality. Why should people work at tasks they hate? A UBI would allow people to attend college, university, or trade school and follow a career they enjoy. It would allow people with children and devote themselves to raising those children – without having to justify their existence to a Social Case Worker, or trying to balance work and home.

However, as noted, people got what they wanted – they have an answer to what they have bemoaned. The death of those over 55 – the death of the Baby-Boomers and last of the Silent Generation – will eliminate Social Security and Medicare recipients and lessen the economic burden on the system. Granted, the majority of those who die are and are likely to remain, male. Women will continue to enjoy the meager benefits, even as the bulk of the recipients die.

Because you wished us (the Silent and Boomer Generations) dead, we can continue to look at how your wish came true.

As we will see in the next chapter, over the first 45 weeks of the two-year comparison, Covid-19 accounts for about 44-percent of the year-to-year change in deaths due to "Natural Causes." Of the usual itemized medical causes, only 11% of the year-to-year change is identified. The remaining 45-percent of Natural Deaths seem to be simply from old age – people reaching a natural expiration date.

On 20 April 1983, Reagan signed legislation to preserve the system and said: *"This bill demonstrates for all time our nation's ironclad commitment to Social Security. ...From this day forward, they have one pledge that they will get their fair share of benefits when they retire."*

The workaround is, if they die, they do not retire. Covid-19 has simply expedited the natural expiration process – again if you believe in prayers and wishes, it is the solution many have desired. When the culling ends, the system will be on a sound footing.

CENTER FOR DISEASE CONTROL & PREVENTION weekly data https://www.cdc.gov/						
Jurisdiction of Occurrence	United States					
MMWR Year	2020					
MMWR Week	1	2	3	4	5	
Week Ending Date	01/04/20	01/11/20	01/18/20	01/25/20	02/01/20	
All Cause	60,155	60,702	59,343	59,144	58,788	
Natural Cause	55,014	55,745	54,520	54,400	54,016	
Septicemia (A40-A41)	846	867	830	828	812	4,183
Malignant neoplasms (C00-C97)	11,567	11,963	11,703	11,877	11,959	59,069
Diabetes mellitus (E10-E14)	1,825	1,939	1,816	1,861	1,824	9,265
Alzheimer disease (G30)	2,528	2,561	2,489	2,511	2,473	12,562
Influenza and pneumonia (J09-J18)	1,558	1,529	1,485	1,487	1,414	7,473
Chronic lower respiratory diseases (J40-J47)	3,500	3,707	3,524	3,395	3,307	17,433
Other diseases of respiratory system	1,065	1,035	992	978	980	5,050
Nephritis, nephrotic syndrome and nephrosis	1,095	1,091	1,124	1,112	1,075	5,497
Symptoms, signs and abnormal clinical and laboratory findings, not elsewhere classified	687	719	685	714	706	3,511
Diseases of heart (I00-I09,I11,I13,I20-I51)	14,190	13,890	13,576	13,595	13,444	68,695
Cerebrovascular diseases (I60-I69)	3,106	3,183	3,252	3,177	3,079	15,797
COVID-19 (U071, Multiple Cause of Death)	1	0	3	2	0	6
COVID-19 (U071, Underlying Cause of Death)	1	0	2	2	0	5

	United States					
	2020					
MMWR Week	6	7	8	9	10	
Week Ending Date	02/08/20	02/15/20	02/22/20	02/29/20	03/07/20	
All Cause	59,367	58,773	58,850	59,260	59,613	
Natural Cause	54,347	53,975	53,991	54,280	54,353	
Septicemia (A40-A41)	811	800	783	820	812	4,026
Malignant neoplasms (C00-C97)	11,693	11,802	11,774	11,782	11,707	58,758
Diabetes mellitus (E10-E14)	1,955	1,841	1,875	1,823	1,859	9,353
Alzheimer disease (G30)	2,505	2,529	2,506	2,518	2,504	12,562
Influenza and pneumonia (J09-J18)	1,462	1,514	1,461	1,509	1,608	7,554
Chronic lower respiratory diseases (J40-J47)	3,400	3,476	3,450	3,451	3,461	17,238
Other diseases of respiratory system	973	978	968	1,009	1,003	4,931
Nephritis, nephrotic syndrome and nephrosis	1,134	1,070	1,054	1,091	1,074	5,423
Symptoms, signs and abnormal clinical and laboratory findings, not elsewhere classified	681	704	714	763	761	3,623
Diseases of heart (I00-I09,I11,I13,I20-I51)	13,971	13,627	13,594	13,679	13,643	68,514
Cerebrovascular diseases (I60-I69)	3,048	3,081	3,077	3,121	3,087	15,414
COVID-19 (U071, Multiple Cause of Death)	1	0	4	10	36	51
COVID-19 (U071, Underlying Cause of Death)	0	0	4	9	32	45

	United States					
	2020					
MMWR Week	11	12	13	14	15	
Week Ending Date	03/14/20	03/21/20	03/28/20	04/04/20	04/11/20	
All Cause	58,642	59,156	62,946	72,238	78,987	
Natural Cause	53,539	54,310	58,223	67,444	73,977	
Septicemia (A40-A41)	765	843	855	945	841	4,249
Malignant neoplasms (C00-C97)	11,569	11,733	11,772	11,592	11,543	58,209
Diabetes mellitus (E10-E14)	1,738	1,827	2,039	2,293	2,348	10,245
Alzheimer disease (G30)	2,437	2,509	2,739	2,863	2,951	13,499
Influenza and pneumonia (J09-J18)	1,635	1,749	1,792	1,870	1,632	8,678
Chronic lower respiratory diseases (J40-J47)	3,380	3,374	3,514	3,536	3,440	17,244
Other diseases of respiratory system	990	1,018	1,061	1,032	1,030	5,131
Nephritis, nephrotic syndrome and nephrosis	1,075	1,102	1,032	1,037	1,123	5,369
Symptoms, signs and abnormal clinical and laboratory findings, not elsewhere classified	762	741	755	843	803	3,904
Diseases of heart (I00-I09,I11,I13,I20-I51)	13,414	13,159	13,678	14,911	15,727	70,889
Cerebrovascular diseases (I60-I69)	3,155	3,059	3,064	3,155	3,187	15,620
COVID-19 (U071, Multiple Cause of Death)	56	573	3,174	10,045	16,209	30,057
COVID-19 (U071, Underlying Cause of Death)	52	537	2,998	9,552	15,409	28,548

	United States					
	2020					
MMWR Week	16	17	18	19	20	
Week Ending Date	04/18/20	04/25/20	05/02/20	05/09/20	05/16/20	
All Cause	76,672	73,800	69,206	66,733	64,386	
Natural Cause	71,851	68,745	64,000	61,283	59,066	
Septicemia (A40-A41)	751	740	739	723	681	3,634
Malignant neoplasms (C00-C97)	11,190	11,352	11,093	11,009	11,259	55,903
Diabetes mellitus (E10-E14)	2,255	2,080	1,926	1,965	1,956	10,182
Alzheimer disease (G30)	2,896	2,801	2,721	2,490	2,430	13,338
Influenza and pneumonia (J09-J18)	1,250	1,158	1,018	869	861	5,156
Chronic lower respiratory diseases (J40-J47)	3,190	2,987	2,920	2,802	2,763	14,662
Other diseases of respiratory system	929	898	858	868	788	4,341
Nephritis, nephrotic syndrome and nephrosis	1,095	987	963	943	979	4,967
Symptoms, signs and abnormal clinical and laboratory findings, not elsewhere classified	824	838	762	844	795	4,063
Diseases of heart (I00-I09,I11,I13,I20-I51)	14,537	13,835	12,966	13,127	12,708	67,173
Cerebrovascular diseases (I60-I69)	3,201	3,054	3,034	2,847	2,957	15,093
COVID-19 (U071, Multiple Cause of Death)	17,093	15,457	13,165	11,185	9,182	66,082
COVID-19 (U071, Underlying Cause of Death)	16,199	14,566	12,376	10,412	8,436	61,989

	United States 2020					
MMWR Week	21	22	23	24	25	
Week Ending Date	05/23/20	05/30/20	06/06/20	06/13/20	06/20/20	
All Cause	61,541	59,568	58,789	57,916	57,859	
Natural Cause	56,106	54,080	53,069	52,396	52,297	
Septicemia (A40-A41)	716	653	731	690	684	3,474
Malignant neoplasms (C00-C97)	11,108	10,899	11,074	11,123	11,144	55,348
Diabetes mellitus (E10-E14)	1,824	1,800	1,713	1,731	1,778	8,846
Alzheimer disease (G30)	2,412	2,261	2,295	2,327	2,354	11,649
Influenza and pneumonia (J09-J18)	809	757	707	693	754	3,720
Chronic lower respiratory diseases (J40-J47)	2,676	2,632	2,559	2,496	2,557	12,920
Other diseases of respiratory system	754	762	779	739	766	3,800
Nephritis, nephrotic syndrome and nephrosis	922	894	907	926	933	4,582
Symptoms, signs and abnormal clinical and laboratory findings, not elsewhere classified	832	846	869	917	943	4,407
Diseases of heart (I00-I09,I11,I13,I20-I51)	12,730	12,391	12,415	12,341	12,322	62,199
Cerebrovascular diseases (I60-I69)	2,818	2,848	2,784	2,839	2,916	14,205
COVID-19 (U071, Multiple Cause of Death)	7,196	6,133	5,012	4,209	3,816	26,366
COVID-19 (U071, Underlying Cause of Death)	6,537	5,552	4,476	3,703	3,329	23,597

United States

2020

	26	27	28	29	30	
Week Ending Date	06/27/20	07/04/20	07/11/20	07/18/20	07/25/20	
All Cause	58,359	59,673	61,738	62,966	64,031	
Natural Cause	52,794	53,950	55,999	57,327	58,600	
Septicemia (A40-A41)	721	686	765	713	691	3,576
Malignant neoplasms (C00-C97)	11,347	11,288	11,312	11,349	11,538	56,834
Diabetes mellitus (E10-E14)	1,757	1,911	1,937	1,875	1,942	9,422
Alzheimer disease (G30)	2,285	2,347	2,462	2,494	2,507	12,095
Influenza and pneumonia (J09-J18)	725	658	732	761	781	3,657
Chronic lower respiratory diseases (J40-J47)	2,529	2,619	2,606	2,636	2,546	12,936
Other diseases of respiratory system	776	779	756	713	722	3,746
Nephritis, nephrotic syndrome and nephrosis	949	985	915	982	968	4,799
Symptoms, signs and abnormal clinical and laboratory findings, not elsewhere classified	967	1,020	1,144	1,208	1,233	5,572
Diseases of heart (I00-I09,I11,I13,I20-I51)	12,427	12,778	12,912	12,759	12,837	63,713
Cerebrovascular diseases (I60-I69)	2,951	2,822	2,908	2,977	2,900	14,558
COVID-19 (U071, Multiple Cause of Death)	3,800	4,497	5,735	7,130	8,156	29,318
COVID-19 (U071, Underlying Cause of Death)	3,293	4,003	5,192	6,471	7,437	26,396

(Row label column: MMWR Week)

	United States 2020					
MMWR Week	31	32	33	34	35	
Week Ending Date	08/01/20	08/08/20	08/15/20	08/22/20	08/29/20	
All Cause	63,973	63,384	63,212	61,998	60,296	
Natural Cause	58,467	57,996	57,891	56,691	55,260	
Septicemia (A40-A41)	688	789	734	739	722	3,672
Malignant neoplasms (C00-C97)	11,498	11,493	11,646	11,447	11,484	57,568
Diabetes mellitus (E10-E14)	1,972	1,773	1,863	1,898	1,840	9,346
Alzheimer disease (G30)	2,492	2,431	2,509	2,548	2,399	12,379
Influenza and pneumonia (J09-J18)	761	773	751	689	671	3,645
Chronic lower respiratory diseases (J40-J47)	2,727	2,576	2,633	2,612	2,520	13,068
Other diseases of respiratory system	781	727	789	777	731	3,805
Nephritis, nephrotic syndrome and nephrosis	958	912	966	959	972	4,767
Symptoms, signs and abnormal clinical and laboratory findings, not elsewhere classified	1,261	1,326	1,388	1,399	1,508	6,882
Diseases of heart (I00-I09,I11,I13,I20-I51)	12,646	12,639	12,647	12,527	12,158	62,617
Cerebrovascular diseases (I60-I69)	2,980	3,018	2,929	2,916	2,947	14,790
COVID-19 (U071, Multiple Cause of Death)	8,237	7,790	7,179	6,292	5,623	35,121
COVID-19 (U071, Underlying Cause of Death)	7,550	7,120	6,499	5,673	5,051	31,893

	United States 2020					
MMWR Week	36	37	38	39	40	
Week Ending Date	09/05/20	09/12/20	09/19/20	09/26/20	10/03/20	
All Cause	58,814	57,540	57,199	58,026	56,843	
Natural Cause	53,729	52,858	52,724	53,750	52,702	
Septicemia (A40-A41)	686	670	717	718	696	3,487
Malignant neoplasms (C00-C97)	11,187	11,116	11,213	11,460	10,948	55,924
Diabetes mellitus (E10-E14)	1,770	1,795	1,742	1,724	1,761	8,792
Alzheimer disease (G30)	2,458	2,266	2,297	2,404	2,315	11,740
Influenza and pneumonia (J09-J18)	723	668	677	687	717	3,472
Chronic lower respiratory diseases (J40-J47)	2,486	2,468	2,407	2,526	2,437	12,324
Other diseases of respiratory system	775	718	762	756	684	3,695
Nephritis, nephrotic syndrome and nephrosis	905	901	879	886	901	4,472
Symptoms, signs and abnormal clinical and laboratory findings, not elsewhere classified	1,589	1,776	1,809	1,997	2,306	9,477
Diseases of heart (I00-I09,I11,I13,I20-I51)	12,042	11,702	11,966	11,969	11,760	59,439
Cerebrovascular diseases (I60-I69)	2,800	2,950	2,835	2,939	2,747	14,271
COVID-19 (U071, Multiple Cause of Death)	4,830	4,389	4,007	4,031	3,940	21,197
COVID-19 (U071, Underlying Cause of Death)	4,271	3,884	3,527	3,543	3,438	18,663

United States						
2020						
MMWR Week	41	42	43	44	45	
Week Ending Date	10/10/20	10/17/20	10/24/20	10/31/20	11/07/20	
All Cause	58,328	56,657	57,578	57,367	58,120	
Natural Cause	54,268	53,045	54,193	54,219	55,253	
Septicemia (A40-A41)	720	710	673	638	661	3,402
Malignant neoplasms (C00-C97)	11,268	10,718	10,956	10,651	10,594	54,187
Diabetes mellitus (E10-E14)	1,751	1,689	1,620	1,704	1,627	8,391
Alzheimer disease (G30)	2,418	2,417	2,443	2,304	2,408	11,990
Influenza and pneumonia (J09-J18)	667	683	715	711	682	3,458
Chronic lower respiratory diseases (J40-J47)	2,455	2,404	2,481	2,344	2,503	12,187
Other diseases of respiratory system	763	772	741	748	718	3,742
Nephritis, nephrotic syndrome and nephrosis	903	949	865	841	871	4,429
Symptoms, signs and abnormal clinical and laboratory findings, not elsewhere classified	2,486	2,483	2,595	2,727	3,131	13,422
Diseases of heart (I00-I09,I11,I13,I20-I51)	11,856	11,412	11,520	11,485	11,288	57,561
Cerebrovascular diseases (I60-I69)	2,954	2,842	2,846	2,872	2,754	14,268
COVID-19 (U071, Multiple Cause of Death)	4,457	4,763	5,445	6,123	7,170	27,958
COVID-19 (U071, Underlying Cause of Death)	3,956	4,215	4,822	5,453	6,431	24,877

	United States 2020					
MMWR Week	46	47	48	49	50	
Week Ending Date	11/14/20	11/21/20	11/28/20	12/05/20	12/12/20	
All Cause	54,002	39,427	55,185	41,676	41,830	
Natural Cause	51,650	38,162	53,034	40,419	40,738	
Septicemia (A40-A41)	606	436	589	458	410	2,499
Malignant neoplasms (C00-C97)	9,825	7,420	9,183	7,174	7,370	40,972
Diabetes mellitus (E10-E14)	1,461	1,103	1,504	1,124	1,088	6,280
Alzheimer disease (G30)	2,307	1,748	2,259	1,872	1,903	10,089
Influenza and pneumonia (J09-J18)	676	503	647	561	555	2,942
Chronic lower respiratory diseases (J40-J47)	2,222	1,677	2,175	1,731	1,824	9,629
Other diseases of respiratory system	698	552	680	556	585	3,071
Nephritis, nephrotic syndrome and nephrosis	808	606	813	651	685	3,563
Symptoms, signs and abnormal clinical and laboratory findings, not elsewhere classified	2,848	2,192	2,835	2,338	2,530	12,743
Diseases of heart (I00-I09,I11,I13,I20-I51)	10,270	7,589	10,012	8,200	8,144	44,215
Cerebrovascular diseases (I60-I69)	2,587	1,930	2,507	2,030	2,115	11,169
COVID-19 (U071, Multiple Cause of Death)	7,465	5,071	10,261	6,301	5,964	35,062
COVID-19 (U071, Underlying Cause of Death)	6,706	4,647	9,314	5,844	5,571	32,082

	United States 2020					
MMWR Week		52		Covid Emerges		
Week Ending Date	12/19/20	12/26/20		Non-Natural Deaths	228,818	
All Cause						
Natural Cause				Covid Dead	262,326	
Septicemia (A40-A41)				NOT Culling	19,807	0
Malignant neoplasms (C00-C97)						0
Diabetes mellitus (E10-E14)				Deaths are NOT cuilling		0
Alzheimer disease (G30)				when there are multiple		0
Influenza and pneumonia (J09-J18)				causes and Covid-19 is		0
Chronic lower respiratory diseases (J40-J47)				not the underlying		0
Other diseases of respiratory system				cause of death. (Did		0
Nephritis, nephrotic syndrome and nephrosis				not serve to expedite		0
Symptoms, signs and abnormal clinical and laboratory findings, not elsewhere classified				the death)		0
Diseases of heart (I00-I09,I11,I13,I20-I51)				TOTAL DEATHS		0
Cerebrovascular diseases (I60-I69)				3,000,656		0
COVID-19 (U071, Multiple Cause of Death)						0
COVID-19 (U071, Underlying Cause of Death)						0

CHAPTER NINE – It's a Curse
"May you live in interesting times.
May you come to the attention of those in authority.
May you find what you are looking for."
~ Origins Unknown, but said to be Chinese

In the classic tale of *The Emperor's New Clothes*, the little boy who shouts out that the Emperor is naked is deemed a fool and a liar by those who have committed to being victims of the "tailor's" fraud.

In the age of Trump and the Covid-19 pandemic, we may well be seeing a similar scenario play out.

As the previous two chapters of factual CDC data shows, the huge numbers connected to the deaths assigned to Covid-19 and those said to be the total deaths from "ALL CAUSES" in 2019 and 2020 do not jive.

This is especially true when, on 4 December, NEWSWEEK published an alleged *"Fact Check"* article by Ken Tarbous entitled: *"Fact Check: Has COVID-19 had no impact on overall US deaths this year?"*

Newsweek's alleged *"Fact Check"* concluded the answer to the question was "False" because *"data from the CDC contradicts the claim, with an estimated 299,028 excess deaths through October 3, including 198,081 (66 percent) attributed to COVID-19."*

In the previous two chapters, I presented you with the data for the period covered by the alleged *"Fact Check"* based on claims about that very same CDC data. Since the *"False"* would seem to go against my persistent claim that Covid-19 is a *"culling virus"* that will only claim those with medical conditions that would probably have killed them within six months to a year, it is important to see if the "Fact Check" {and CDC spokesman quoted} is telling the truth or is a liar.

Curiously, in the Trump-era, the honesty and accuracy of Fact Checkers are controlling the nation's choice in leadership and global events. This is not to say [which I have already said] that Biden was destined to defeat Trump, the reality of the POTUS

Cousins and 4-Sisters dictates that he was – just as Trump was destined to defeat Clinton because she was {ancestrally} unrelated to the 4-Sisters.

LOL. It is, after all, how Satan exercises his right to Vote – or carry out divine design.

If you believe in such things.

If you don't, then the POTUS Cousins and 4-Sisters become what can be termed an interesting pattern of coincidence or sub-rosa animal behavior concerning the selection of the "lead stallion" or "lion king".

The "Fact Check" article tells us: *"The story was published on November 22, then taken down, with a retraction published on November 27. The retraction said the study cited in the story 'has been used to support dangerous inaccuracies that minimize the impact of the pandemic.'"*

It also claimed that the basis for the retraction was that there were: *"300,000 excess deaths attributed to COVID-19, as of early October, according to Centers for Disease Control and Prevention (CDC) data."*

The statement was, to put it mildly, pure bullshit.

It exaggerates the number of Covid-19 connected deaths by 100,000 – and they are not "excess deaths," they are the normal deaths attributable to the death of members of both the Silent and Boomer generations.

Moreover, these numbers will continue to accelerate – those who silent generation {like Nancy Pelosi} have seriously exceeded their anticipated mortality – her generation was expected to die by age 69 and she was still going at 80.

We have the CDC numbers, the deaths from all causes and those for natural causes, as well as the 2020 deaths assigned to the Coronavirus, for the first 45-weeks of both 2019 and 2020. In 2019, the first 45-weeks ended on 15 November, and in 2020, it ended on 13 November.

However, if we look at the chart at the end of Chapter 7, we see that the CDC spokesperson is speaking about the first 40-weeks or first eight 5-week periods on the charts where the average period had an increase of about 59,600 and the overall deaths were up an average of 46,100. But that is fully consistent with the age group involved and those numbers are due to climb – even if, as Eric Trump asserted on 17 May, *"coronavirus will magically, all of the sudden, go away and disappear...."*

That means we need to take another look at that chart but in terms of total deaths rather than the average difference per 5-week period.

However, we still have the same problem of the increase in total deaths being less than the increase in natural causes deaths – which includes the Covid-19.

Phrased another way, while the deaths from natural causes were increased, the reaction to the pandemic caused a significant decrease in accidents and other non-natural causes.

As has been observed, the phenomenon has also manifested itself as improved in the air – because the pandemic has forced a change in normal human behavioral activities associated with air pollution.

According to the charts in Chapter 8, the deaths start to show when, in week 13 of 2020, the Covid-19 deaths reach 3,174 – the following week they exceed 10,000, and the week after that they exceed 16,000. Still, as the second chart shows, after 45 weeks the number of Covid-19 related deaths was 236,156 NOT 300,000. It follows that, in October, the number was less than 200,000.

On 2 December, the nation set a single-day record of 2,804 deaths of individuals with fatal conditions complicated by Covid-19. Experts responded by predicting a death toll of 450,000 would be possible by the end of February, even though vaccinations were due to begin mid-December; in Northern Ireland and Wales, they would begin at 8 A.M. on 8 December.

As seen on the chart on page 112, the Covid-19 death toll for those five-week period was about 28,000; there four, the 12-weeks ending 27 February could reasonably add 67,200 to the roughly 280,000 dead when the expert opinion was rendered – meaning the total would likely be less than 350,00 and not the more pessimistic 450,000. A possibility that could explain why Biden has announced he would be replacing that expert, Dr. Robert Redfield, with the head of infectious diseases at Massachusetts

General Hospital, and Harvard Professor Of Medicine, Rochelle Walensky.

Because we are dealing with a culling virus, the White House coronavirus response coordinator, Dr. Deborah Birx, warned *"So if you have anyone in your family with co-morbidities or over 70, you cannot do those things. You cannot gather with your mask off, you cannot hug and kiss people outside."*

Curiously, the Newsweek chart shows age 65 to 74 as the first high mortality group, so shouldn't it be *"or over 65"*?

The alleged "Fact Check" was based on what could be politely termed an exaggeration and realistically a blatant lie that would not come close to being true for nearly three months.

Above, I included a variation on the Chapter 7 chart that has the actual total, rather than the average for the nine weekly periods for which there is data at the time of this writing. Below, we have yet another chart that focuses on the standard medical issues that fall in the *"Natural Cause"* category.

Note that two categories went negative – one is cell growth associated with tumors, "Malignant Neoplasm"; the other is

United States Deaths in 2019		United States Deaths in 2020	
All Causes	Natural	All Causes	Natural
291,654	268,331	298,132	273,695
291,676	267,920	295,863	270,946
284,384	260,763	331,969	307,493
269,776	246,388	350,797	324,945
265,209	240,515	295,673	267,948
235,058	180,283	306,767	278,670
232,057	177,506	312,863	286,305
236,275	180,058	288,422	265,763
247,395	188,059	288,050	270,978
2,353,484 Total	2,009,823	2,768,536 Total	2,546,743
Comparing first 45 weeks of 2019 and 2020			
415,052 All	{2020 less 2019}	Natural	536,920

| United States Deaths | | | |
| First 45 Weeks of Year (end 19 or 7 November) | | | |
YEAR	2019	2020	CHANGE
Septicemia (A40-A41)	32,960	33,703	743
Malignant neoplasms (C00-C97)	518,136	511,800	(6,336)
Diabetes mellitus (E10-E14)	75,069	83,842	8,773
Alzheimer disease (G30)	103,200	111,814	8,614
Influenza and pneumonia (J09-J18)	42,979	46,813	3,834
Chronic lower respiratory diseases (J40-J47)	135,074	130,012	(5,062)
Other diseases of respiratory system	37,774	38,241	467
Nephritis, nephrotic syndrome and nephrosis	44,132	44,305	173
Symptoms, signs and abnormal clinical and laboratory findings, not elsewhere classified	27,047	54,861	27,814
Diseases of heart (I00-I09,I11,I13,I20-I51)	565,959	580,800	14,841
Cerebrovascular diseases (I60-I69)	128,206	134,016	5,810
COVID-19 (U071, Multiple Cause of Death)	0	236,156	236,156
COVID-19 (U071, Underlying Cause of Death)	0	216,013	216,013
Natural Cause	2,009,823	2,546,743	536,920
All Cause	2,353,484	2,768,536	415,052

Chronic Lower Respiratory Disease. Also, note that there was a doubling in the category of abnormal clinical and laboratory findings. This could indicate there are yet to be discovered medical conditions that are being exposed by Covid-19 as part of the culling process.

The important thing to note is that Coronavirus is associated with "*Multiple Cause of Death*" and, within that classification, as an "*Underlying Cause of Death*" – which is the "culling" or catalyst that triggers the real cause of death or illness.

Over the 45-periods covered in the chart, deaths from "*Natural Causes*" increased by over a half-million, while the overall deaths increased by an amount that was 20-percent lower.

Regardless, the "*as of early October*" statement must be seen as a bald-faced lie.

What the unidentified spokesperson for the CDC was credited with stating was that "*as of early October*" the CDC was claiming more deaths than the 285,786 official count on 5 December 2020 – that is, there were more total deaths for the year in early October than there were two months later, in early DECEMBER.

What happened? Did they come back to life?

Or are we seeing another example of the MSM lies that have dogged Trump's factual statements and rational, business-judgment based, behavior?

Are we to panic because, in the 45-weeks, deaths were up?

The first members of the Baby-Boomer generation tuned 75 in 2020. This was a generation born into families who smoked, where lead-based paint was commonly used in every home, and where the range of unhealthy activities was considered normal.

We also need to recognize that the remaining members of the Silent Generation are generally overdue for death. They do not need the Coronavirus to add them to the rolls.

Taken together, the number of people who die every year is on a steady rise and will continue to rise until around the year 2035 when most of them will be gone. The Baby-Bust means that, while the percentage of the population who die will doubtless remain constant, the number will decrease.

In keeping with the spirit of "Satan's Vote" and the mystical forces popular among a large segment of the population, we should keep in mind the Book of Revelation prophecy that a third of life is going to die in this era.

A third of life means that portion of the 7.8 billion people who now populate the world, about 28-percent of which are Baby-Boomers, and the range of animals who are being driven to extinct by Climate Change.

According to the Census Bureau, we can expect *"Data from the 2020 Census will show the impact of the baby boomers on America's population age structure."* We already have evidence that, because of the Baby-Bust, their share of the population has grown from *"12.4% in 2000 to 16.0% in 2018"* and the census is likely to show they are now 20% of the United States population.

Those who are not culled by the Coronavirus could easily live into their 80s. And that is far more important than the focus on the number of cases – it is the number of deaths that will introduce the economic and social forces shaping the next three decades. And are the forces being ignored?

The Coronavirus has shown that we need to have a Universal Basic Income that is above poverty and reliable. The reliability will serve to bolster the economy and must start with a minimum Social Security benefit that is above poverty and free of the need for the supplements in the form of the Supplemental Nutrition Assistance Program (SNAP, which was known as Food Stamps before it went to the digital EBT card), and Low Income Home Energy Assistance Program (LIHEAP).

Bernie Sanders and the Progressives talk about Medicare for All (M4A), which is simply an expansion of the existing program that comes with Social Security. As it is in Canada, Western Europe, and other advanced nations, medical coverage should be a universal right provided by the government in the same way the government provides basic 12-year education.

Coronavirus and the related stimulus packages have shown both the wisdom and need for basic economic and health support. In the years to come, Climate Change will prove to be a catalyst for the introduction of new and deadly pandemics or plagues. It is thus necessary that the nation learns from the current experience and uses that learning to insulate or shield itself from what could prove to be far worse.

In the spirit of Satan's Vote, we are being shown what we need to do and what is expected of us if we wish the nation and our children to survive this century.

There are other lessons the United States should be learning. One is what the Asian nations have known for decades – wearing masks during flu season, or whenever there is an acute respiratory illness circulating through the population, is the wise thing to do.

A research paper submitted on 28 July 2020 and approved for PNAS publication on 10 November 2020, entitled, *"Face masks considerably reduce COVID-19 cases in Germany"*, reported: *"that face masks reduced the number of newly registered severe acute respiratory syndrome coronavirus 2 infections between 15% and 75% over a period of 20 days after their mandatory introduction."*

Based on the study data, it was estimated that *"face masks reduce the daily growth rate of reported infections by around*

47%."

On 3 December, President-elect Biden stated that he plans to call on Americans to wear masks for his first 100 days in office. This would not be a mandatory act, but, as Biden said, *"Just 100 days to mask, not forever. 100 days. And I think we'll see a significant reduction"* in the Coronavirus contamination.

Biden went on to state: *"It's time to end the politicization of basic, responsible public health steps like mask-wearing and social distancing. A mask is not a political statement, but it is a good way to start pulling the country together."*

The wearing of masks during flu season is a lesson Americans need to learn and become comfortable with. Economically, the use of masks has become a growth industry. And, as people adapt, they will learn about such add-ons as mask brackets which fit between the wearer's mouth and the mask to create a space that makes it easier to talk and breath, while also reducing the annoyance of eye-glass fogging that is common with the basic masks available in many stores. The silicone frame has an added advantage for women – it prevents lipstick smudging.

Of course, there are the expensive masks that have a frame-like structure designed into them. But they are harder to come by and not as practical for use by children. And we want our children and grandchildren to learn to be comfortable using these protective garments.

As a growth industry, the production of customized masks is already emerging among firms in the photo-print service industry. Here again, there is an opportunity for children to acquire a custom mask of their own design. And Biden's position will help grow this *"Social Distance"* industry.

Biden's mask initiative followed reports that the previous day saw a single-day record number of Coronavirus deaths – more than 2,800 – and, as previously mentioned, the CDC director has stated: *"The reality is December and January and February are going to be rough times. I actually believe they're going to be the most difficult time in the public health history of this nation."*

With that comes the potential for serious economic problems for the nation, problems that House Speaker Nancy Pelosi seems happy to impose on the new administration.

If she weren't, she would have already pushed a stripped-down stimulus that would deliver another cash allotment to citizens who received the previous $1,200 payment, and also extend the unemployment assistance to all those places of employment are closed due to the pandemic.

However, when the financial legislation finally passes – with only $600 per person – Trump made it clear he wanted it to provide $2,000, and Pelosi immediately jumped on the amendment train. But, playing Scrooge, House Minority Leader Kevin McCarthy made it clear he would block the Speaker's attempt to pass an amendment via unanimous consent. And on 24 December he kept that promise.

Pelosi's plan to seek passage via unanimous consent had one objective – to ensure it wouldn't pass while providing the optics of her attempting what Trump and the Progressives were calling for.

Had Pelosi really wanted the Bill to pass, she it would have by a strict party-line majority vote was the way to go.

Pelosi ensured the amendment would fail and we can expect Trump will pocket veto the Bill and trigger a Government shutdown – making the waste represented by billions for foreign governments a matter for Biden to address. One issue is $1.3 Billion for Egypt to purchase Russian weapons or military supplies – but, the survival of Americans and the economy is only worth $900 million.

If the Swamp Denizens had their way, America would step into an era of darkness. As Charles Dickens said: *"There are dark shadows on the earth, but its lights are stronger in the contrast."*

Will Biden ignite those stronger lights?

Trump did when he made it clear he wanted a larger stimulus amount – one that was in line with what the Progressives were calling for.

Can Biden-46 reverse the darkness, put aside the incessant attacks on Trump, and return the nation to an era of unprecedented growth and prosperity that had been put on hold by Coronavirus?

We are under a timeless curse of appearances over substance – will Biden bend to the appearance, will he take on the role of one who is "Presidential," or will he be a leader?

Again we can turn to Dickens who, during the Victorian era, observed that *"Dignity, and even holiness too, sometimes, are more questions of coat and waistcoat than some people imagine."*

Trump has been denounced because he has strived to live a Dickens-type existence – an existence in which all is possible. One where *"The most important thing in life is to stop saying 'I wish' and start saying 'I will.' Consider nothing impossible, then treat possibilities as probabilities."*

As the nation moved from election day to Thanksgiving and then started the approach to an unusual Christmas holiday season, Charles Dickens and "A Christmas Carol" take on a meaning that might well have made Dickens laugh.

It has been 177-years since Dickens introduced us to money-grubbing Ebenezer Scrooge who proclaimed, *"Bah! Humbug!"* and dismissed the poor as fit only for workhouses or death – to decrease the surplus population in an era when the global population was about one-seventh of what it is in 2020.

Ebenezer Scrooge was a merchant who ran a counting-house – an accountant dealing in the exchange of money, he might well have been a Christian variation on Shakespeare's Shylock – in their respective eras, both men were merchant-bankers and financiers. They were then, as their counterparts are now, representatives of the Biblical Tribe of Zebulun.

In the Biblical, the role of Zebulun is to provide support for the Scholarly Tribe Issachar. In our modern Biden-era, we hear calls for a return to that pairing – you might recognize it as the call for free college tuition and college loan forgiveness.

In our modern era, Christmas has moved from a minor observance to the peak mercantile season of the year. Christmas is the season of Scrooge – the season when most retail profits, the true annual profit, for the year are generated.

As we move into that season, the unique changes caused by the reaction to the Coronavirus and seen online retail profits expand and the demand for devices to access online services soar. Hi-tech Scrooges are making money, and politicians like Elizabeth Warren and AOC's Squad are denouncing them for it, while also wanting them to take on the obligations allotted to the Tribe of

Zebulun.

That denunciation goes over well with those who also would denounce Scrooge and Shylock, those who are trained to respond to the dog whistle that rouses the peasants and brings down the Kings.

Warren, Pelosi, and the rest have amassed their millions by yelling to the mobs that a millionaire's profits are wrong. They are happy to attack Trump, who suffered losses and still made profits by producing things of value to both the community and the nation. It is somehow logical that the politician's millions should benefit only themselves.

Satan has voted, and those who play games with money to support the average person being harmed by Covid-19 expect to be rewarded for the additional harm they are inflicting. Yet, as the 2020 election showed, the people are getting wise to the two-faced game and so we saw Blue Districts Turn Red, even as the rules that govern POTUS Cousins and descendants of the 4-Sisters remained in play.

We can watch the media denounce Trump for claiming that he "won" the election. He didn't and, if the nation was to survive, he couldn't have – that is the magical charm associated with those nations run by POTUS Cousin descendants of the 4-Sisters.

But Trump does adhere to a Dickens' claim, "*I have been bent and broken, but – I hope – into a better shape.*" Or, at least we will see what happens if rationality and concern for the nation emerge in a Washington defined by the Biden-era.

Satan's Vote is either a curse or a blessing. If a curse, then we will see that Wall Street was wrong to view the election outcome as a positive warranting new height in the financial markets – those are the root of prosperity for retirement accounts and family assets.

While the older generation will be culled, the result will be some sorrow, but also relief from many medical costs that only serve to extend a life that can no longer be properly lived and enjoyed.

For those who knew how to enjoy and experience life, being confined to a nursing home or intensive care facility is a curse. Yet, there are those for whom a nursing home, or senior care facility has become a blessing – a place of companionship among those of the same generation, those who have lost or are separated from their loved ones.

Again, as Dickens described his, and our, time:

"*...the best of times, ...worst of times, ...the age of wisdom, ...of foolishness, ...the epoch of belief, ...of incredulity, ...the season of light, ...of darkness, ...the spring of hope, ...the winter of despair.*"

CHAPTER TEN – VAXXER World

"I do think that a system that allows billionaires to exist when there are parts of Alabama where people are still getting ringworm because they don't have access to public health is wrong."
~ Congresswoman Alexandria Ocasio-Cortez

Throughout the Trump Card series, I have referred to truths or observations continually proven to be accurate. Americans have lived through four years of attacks on Trump, and the basis of those attacks is that he is not playing by the con-artist rules that have controlled Washington and the history of politics in general.

It has been said, *PT "Barnum's great discovery was not how easy it was to deceive the public, but rather, how much the public enjoyed being deceived."* And, since his discovery or realization, not much has changed. The Impeachment demonstrated that the public still loves to be deceived – my much-cited *"Overwhelming evidence"* without a statutory crime to associate with it, is an ideal example of how the dishonest deceive a public that is both willing and deeply desirous to be deceived.

As I cited on page 95 of book 2, H.L. Mencken is credited with saying: *"Nobody ever went broke underestimating the intelligence of the American public {or voter}."*

We see many within the mainstream media {MSM} receiving six-figure incomes because they are taking full advantage of viewer ignorance as a source of profit – as her quote tells us, AOC wants to deprive media representatives of their ill-gotten gains.

Or is she foolish enough to believe she can actually tap into Hi-Tech gains and not detrimentally affect the economy and nation as a whole? Has she never heard of the *Laffer Curve* and what high taxes did to Britain in the 1970s – but then, she was born in 1989 and so, that was both before her time; even costly dial-up services like AOL were only six-years-old when she was born.

Phineas Taylor Barnum {1810-1891}, Henry Louis Mencken {1880-1956} and, of course, Adolph Hitler's {1889-1945} "simpleton masses" are variations on the same voter classification grouping. It is amazing, and yet historically documented, how people will happily disregard that which is visible and in-their-face – *"The Emperor's New Clothes"* {1837} are seen by the fools who do not want to be revealed as fools; they desire membership in the stampeding herd of lemmings heading over the nearest cliff.

Looking back in the series, to page 90 of book 1, we find that Barnum explained a reality we heard about from Teddy Roosevelt and saw poorly implemented with Obama's *"Affordable Care Act"*:

"The foundation of success in life is good health: that is the substratum fortune; it is also the basis of happiness. A person cannot accumulate a fortune very well when he is sick."

A curious aspect of health is longevity – how many years will we clock before we expire? A longer life allows more experience and that experience is a form of learning, and learning adds years to the life of the average person. Practical education and formal education add to longevity – the ignorant or poor thinkers tend to die young.

With the pandemic, researchers have theorized that remote learning, as it currently exists, take months or, possibly, years off the life expectancy of our children and grandchildren. Sadly, before we know how accurate the theories are, the children will need to reach the end of their life cycles.

Are we willing to risk the theory proving to be factual?

Or should we amend Barnum's observation to say that the foundation of success is good health and the best possible education available? Should we strive to give all our children the resources to go as far in school as their intellect will allow?

We began with grade schools; then we provided them with free secondary or high school education; it's time we added another two to four years to the state-sponsored learning experience – let all children strive to be among the elite one-percent and allow an elite one-percent to define the average American citizen with respect to all others on the planet. In the process, America may become the nation with a historically longer life expectancy – it could attain the Biblical 120-years.

But again, where the 'American Dream' is to amass a fortune, the AOC vision of America is to deny or punish that dream. And it is in that context that Trump has been attacked for being the third generation in a family that has sought to, and achieved, some degree of that dream.

But AOC goes further. She hates that America is built on "*a system that allows billionaires to exist.*" But if it weren't for that system, would Henry Ford or Walter Chrysler have been able to create the "Big Three" automobile companies that put Detroit on the map? Would there be a Microsoft, Apple, or Amazon? And without them would there be anything approaching the social media world AOC utilizes to reach her fan-base?

Only those who want America to fail, who have wanted DJT to fail – both as a President and as a World Leader – would oppose ensuring Americans have the best healthcare system in the world or denigrate those who have achieved the 'American Dream' and are now a role model for the next generation of creative innovators.

Look around. While Trump boasts of America being a global leader in the export of fossil fuel, in the period during which he encouraged those exports, America also took enormous strides in the production and use of renewable energy.

As the Biblical advice says, do not judge by their words, judge by their deeds – by the fruits. As symbolized by the words of AOC and Bernie Sanders, Congress has produced many words, but no fruit can be found. They want America to be part of an agreement, a Paris Climate Accord, that cannot possibly achieve anything within any reasonable timeframe – the signatories have simply moved their pollutants offshore to non-signatory nations.

The fossil fuel industry has long received subsidies, depletion allowances, and multiple tax-breaks that encourage its destruction of the planet. It has been encouraged to engage in fracking – which, since the 1960s, has been proved to cause earthquakes and other environmental disruptions.

But when DJT suggested the southern border wall also be a solar field – a platform for renewable solar energy – he was attacked by the Progressives and those who should have jumped at the opportunity by allowing him his duel purpose wall.

But, they do not want that.

Were Congress to seriously encourage renewable energy on such an enormous scale, it would create more billionaires – and AOC has made it clear that the system should not allow billionaires to exist.

It is far better that we deplete our fossil fuels, and have no alternative in place. How else could America to become dependent on foreign energy and therefore as militarily weak as Germany in 1944/45? How else could the nation be placed in the position of having to engage in a Middle Eastern war for oil in 2033?

Four years ago, on page 185 of book 1, you were told that the Trump plan was to see that, *"From this moment on, it's going to be America First. Every decision on trade, on taxes, on immigration, on foreign affairs, will be made to benefit American workers and American families."*

But, as we have seen with the handling of the second stimulus package, the last thing the anti-Trump forces want to achieve is *"to benefit American workers and American families."*

As of 8 December, there was a bipartisan agreement on a $908 billion package that would deny voters another $1,200 check. As noted, Trump then repeated his agreement with Progressives that there should be a $2,000 check.

The Swamp Denizens had argued that while America is the richest nation on Earth – possibly in history – in terms of economic support for its citizens, it is far from the top and, while it can afford to fund Egypt buying Russian military supplies which might be used to kill American allies, it afford monthly payments to those it has denied the right to work.

In April, Americans received $1,200. Eight months later, a meager $600 more was offered – meaning the average taxpayer is worth less than $150 a month when they are locked out of their jobs and threatened with poverty that is NOT supplemented by public assistance.

However, bad-and-nasty European socialist states have shown they can provide monthly payments: "Australia {$1,993}; Canada {$1,433}; Denmark {$3,288}; France {$7,575}; Germany {$7,327}; Ireland {$1,794}; The UK {$3,084}. Interestingly, the UK can manage payments while also going through economic recession complications related to BREXIT.

That is a clear failure of Congress – of Pelosi, Schumer, and McConnell – to care for the average working and retired American.

We cannot blame Trump – he's been advocating economic growth for America and a $2,000 check. He's also opposed the use of American resources to support nations that wish us harm.

No! It is on Pelosi and those in the House of Representatives – both Democrat and Republican – who are the Swamp Denizens that have been working to enrich or empower themselves.

Progressives became very vocal in their complaints, and even Republicans called for Trump to veto any legislation that failed to include a meaningful second installment.

On 4 December, Alexandria Ocasio-Cortez @AOC Tweeted:

"Canada did $2,000/monthly. The US is the richest nation on earth and a 2nd stimulus check is getting blocked [because the] GOP want corporate bailouts & austerity in 'exchange' for it. Maybe if everyone in the US incorporated as an LLC, Mitch McConnell would actually do something for them."

Of course, AOC is ignoring the problem that it was the huge Nancy Pelosi refusing to consider any relief bill less than $2 Trillion – stuffed with her irrelevant pork legislative agenda – that delayed things to the last minute.

Back in early October, Pelosi and her House Democrats were insisting on a $2.2 trillion "coronavirus relief" bill stuffed with all kinds of political agenda issues that had nothing at all to do with the realities of the pandemic.

One analysis called it *"a left-wing wish list."* To some degree it was – at least it was "a left-wing Swamp Denizen wish list" that sought to change election laws: Barring voter ID requirements; forcing states to count any-and-all absentee ballots that arrive up to ten days after the election; with a requirement that all states allow same-day voter registration. In short, enhancing the probability of future election fraud.

That last requirement is cute. Same-day registration would enable individuals to spend election day traveling between polling places, registering and voting as often as their travel schedule would allow – the nature of such a process affords poll watchers no means of verifying the individual's eligibility or residency in the district.

For California, this means they could reward undocumented

individuals who illegally vote in highly contested districts.

The funds Pelosi sought included $220 billion for teachers union protection. There was another $417 billion for a city and state slush fund and an additional $600 billion for cities and states to use to plug budgetary holes resulting from fiscal incompetence. It even included $5 billion designated as "flexible resource" funds which would be pocket money for local politicians.

Pure California pork that had the added benefit of ensuring there would be no legislation before the election – nothing Trump could point to as an accomplishment of his administration. Pelosi did not and, while she remains House Speaker, will not do anything to help the average American citizen. Though she will go out of her way to seek ways to import undocumented bodies to gerrymander the size of Southern California districts and enhance the size of her California Congressional delegation.

While Pelosi and Schumer play their childish political games, across the nation, the average citizen will be hurting. Comically, in New York, Los Angeles, and San Francisco, the businesses which give those cities their unique character were being forced to close. The citizens who elected Schumer and Pelosi are being intentionally hurt by a forced economic shutdown justified by a virus that seems to specifically attack those who are retired and not part of the day-to-day economy.

And putting aside the workers as victims – who could easily be protected by masks and a degree of workplace social distancing – politically, actions by Pelosi and Schumer are going to undermine the Biden-Harris administration before they even assume office.

As of 8 December, the possibility of another stimulus check appears to be something that will emerge from a different piece of legislation that is passed sometime after Biden is sworn in. But, by that time, there will be irreparable damage to the economy.

Again we have the comical aspect. The only salvation for an economy that has been so effectively undermined is to build a new foundation based on a universal income.

As has been stated earlier, a UBI not only makes economic sense because of the costly programs it eliminates and replaces, but it will shield the nation from the effects of the next pandemic. One such possible "next" was reported in Southern India.

On 8 December it was reported that over 300 residents of the southern Indian state of Andhra Pradesh were hospitalized on the 5th and 6th of December after reporting *"symptoms similar to those associated with epilepsy, including headaches, nausea, vomiting, and seizures."*

Unlike Coronavirus, this mysterious illness does not appear to target a specific age group or those with pre-existing potentially fatal conditions. One thing they have established is that *"all the patients brought in with the epilepsy-like symptoms had tested negative for COVID-19."*

Throughout the books in this series, whenever the subject of Climate Change arose I have warned that equatorial regions will give rise to new diseases that will eventually be carried north by climate migrants. As of this writing, there is no data on the nature or cause of this new *"epilepsy-like"* illness.

As a general guide, I designated a region between 15 degrees north and south latitude as the Western hemisphere area of focus for any possible future pandemic or plague that might affect United States territory. The Indian region of Andhra Pradesh is situated just within, on the cusp of northern latitude boundary designation. The specific location of the outbreak is Eluru city, which is situated at 16°42 42″N.

On 8 December, India's 1,385,900,954 population reported 9,735,975 cases of Covid-19 and 141,398 deaths equating to 0.7% of their population and 1.5% of their cases. In contrast, 4.7% of the US population was reported to have the virus and of those, 1.9% died. Globally, the reported death rate was three percent.

In New Delhi, the burning season has begun, which means their air pollution will be on the rise. and a grey-orange gloom of deathly annual smog will be hanging over its residents – ensuring its place on the list of the world's most polluted cities.

In 2019, the global deaths from air pollution numbered 6.67 million; India accounted for 1.67 million of them. Over 80-percent of India's cities struggle with unhealthy air quality and account for 21 out of the world's top 30 most polluted cities. It follows that Covid-19 would be a minor secondary cause of death in India.

In the United States, the regions that had the most Covid-19 deaths have also been those with the most air pollution – though the type of pollution is sufficiently different from that found in India is an underlying immunological stress factor common among the older generation raised in the days when homes were still heated with coal or wood and smoking was common.

As readers might know, 8 December became an important date in Covid-19 history, apart from being the day when Margaret Keenan, an age 90 British citizen, became the first person to receive the new vaccine; thereby beginning the British inoculation campaign to alleviate Britain's Coronavirus problem which had claimed less than one-tenth of one percent of its population of 68 million people.

Upon receiving the first shot of the two vaccine protocol, Margaret said: *"It's the best early birthday present I could wish for because it means I can finally look forward to spending time with my family and friends in the new year after being on my own for most of the year."*

Given it was Britain, it is interesting that the second person vaccinated was an 81-year-old man named William Shakespeare.

With Britain now the first western nation to begin a mass vaccination program, Russia announced it would begin vaccinating doctors and teachers on the 12th – using its own Sputnik V.

In the United States, final approval of the Pfizer vaccine used in Britain was scheduled to be addressed at a U.S. Food and Drug Administration committee meeting scheduled on the 10th; after that approval, it was anticipated there would be receipt of 6.4 million doses, enough to innoculate 3.1 million people, available before the end of 2020.

But, on the 7th, the New York Times reported that officials had passed on an earlier Pfizer offer to sell the U.S. additional doses of the yet to be approved vaccine. Instead, the administration held to the original July commitment to purchase 100 million doses of the unproven vaccine for $1.95 billion.

A second vaccine, developed by Moderna, is also likely to be granted emergency approval, and officials have stated there are a possible five other vaccines in the approval cue.

As of this writing, the Pfizer vaccine, developed in association with BioNTech – the German firm whose work was funded by the German government – is the only one scheduled for widespread use in Britain, Canada, and the United States.

The German government is still in a process of establishing the logistical details of their mass vaccination program. With a population of about 84 million people, Germany has reported only about 20 thousand deaths.

On 8 December, Biden, in his first speech addressing specific pandemic related policies, claimed, *"it is possible that after 100 days, we will be much farther along in the fight against the pandemic."*

Referring to Covid-19 as "a mass casualty event," he classified it as the nation's leading cause of death. And while that could be true, given the demographic it harms, the reality is that it is simply a variation on the nation's true leading cause of death – having a medical condition while being of an age that qualifies you to collect Social Security benefits.

Among those in the stage with Biden was California Attorney General Xavier Becerra (D), a former 12-term House member and supporter of Medicare-for-All, who is now the first Latino and the first top state legal official ever designated as a nominee for Secretary of the Department of Health and Human Services.

While the others introduced to address medical issues are medical professionals, Becerra is a legal expert with experience addressing that category of national medical issues -- the important area of navigating legal minefields and challenges to the system that is vital to go well-being of the nation.

Remember PT Barnum's assertion that good health is critical to prosperity. Ideally, Becerra will ensure that every American will have the health that grants access to the opportunity to prosper. Though we can be assured, the Swamp Denizens will object.

It is worth noting that, during his time in the House, Becerra sat on the Ways and Means Committee, which has jurisdiction over the government's health insurance programs and was highly active in the Affordable Care Act process, as well as its subsequent defense.

While, not being a doctor, he lacks first-hand knowledge of medical procedures, having that knowledge would not enhance the ability to deal with the managerial logistics that define the role of Secretary of the Department of Health and Human Services.

Within the current highly adversarial environment, someone lacking Becerra's experience would actually be a detriment. The one in charge of DHHS need not know how to write a prescription or use a stethoscope, they need experience talking to Congressman and other professional political types, as well as having knowledge of the various applicable laws.

Whoever is the DHHS Secretary will also need to implement the logistics associated with Biden Covid-19 policies. They are going to need to ensure Biden doesn't look the fool – especially given his 8 December pledge of '*100 million shots in 100 days*' beginning when he assumes office on 20 January 2021.

Given what we know, at the time of this writing, that's a lie, an impossible goal or objective. As stated, 6.4 million doses were to be received by the end of the year; the two inoculation protocol means those would be gone by the end of February; given the current production schedule, it will be June or July before Biden can even obtain those 100 million doses.

The only possible way he can have them administered in the first 100 days he's in office is by relying upon the promised delivery date for the initial Trump order – meaning Biden plans to take credit for Trump's 'Operation Warp Speed' accomplishment. At the same time, Trump has stated vaccines should come to the United States, and fulfill its needs, before any further distribution in other counties – indicating Biden is relying upon Trump to that pull-off.

Biden has prefaced his stated inoculation goal with a logical logistic problem that can only be deemed a boldfaced political lie.

In the perverse world we now live in, commitments like the one Biden so boldly made are what symbolize that, even as he lost the election, Trump has won – he's being proven right concerning the prevailing realities.

Granted, those who so proudly love to praise "The Emperor's New Clothes" will neither see nor hear what I am saying – they will simply live the reality and wonder what happened.

Using his traditional, "common enemy" political tone, Biden said: *"Out of our collective pain, we are going to find a collective purpose. To control the pandemic, to save lives and to heal as a nation."* And he promised the nation would see the *"most efficient mass vaccination plan in US history."* At the same time, he made it a point to downplay Trump's 'War Speed" by saying, *"developing a vaccine is only one herculean task; distributing it is another."*

Biden also covered his line by setting the stage to blame the outgoing Congress for what will be the failure to deliver in January the vaccines that cannot arrive before June. He looked to the House and Senate – imploring them to pass a coronavirus economic relief package that included the financial resources his administration would need to distribute the vaccines (he is not going to have).

He said, lacking those financial resources could dramatically *"slow and stall"* the distribution process. But, Biden is also aware that masks work – Japan and China routinely use them against the flu, just as they were used in 1918. Accordingly, he has called for a hundred days of mask-wearing and suggested he'd be imposing the mandatory use of masks on trains, buses, and planes crossing state lines; wearing them would also be required in Federal buildings.

On 10 December, a deaths-per-million measurement showed New Jersey leading the nation, then New York, Massachusetts, Connecticut, and Louisiana.

In total deaths, New York has held onto that leadership slot, followed by Texas, California, Florida, and New Jersey. Of the five, only New Jersey is not also in the top five in state population – in that grouping, it falls to 11th place and is replaced in the top five by Pennsylvania {which is 7th in deaths}.

Several patterns that can be derived from a top-five ranking system. California, Texas, and Florida are the most populous states in the Union. Florida can be characterized as Latino and Elderly retirees from Northeast Corridor New England states.

These states are also transportation hubs with commerce connections linked to their population size and the source of huge amounts of air pollution. They are basically a locus point for illness.

The culling will end, as the vaccinations take effect.

But there is a possible series of long-term benefits to be derived from changes in attitudes caused both by the virus and the Congressional economic response.

People who did not know poverty are now experiencing it as an imposed force or penalty associated with the type of leadership that existed prior to Trump's administration.

Trump's approach to the economy and international trade had exposed them to record prosperity, and then knew the reality of suddenly being forced into poverty by an uncaring government that considers all who have no money to be *"Welfare Queens"* or *lazy*. The effect is to open their eyes to the benefit of Progressive economic and medical support.

CHAPTER ELEVEN – Elephant in Room
"The harsh reality is that there is 1000 times more evidence of the Bidens being compromised by China than there ever was about the Trumps and Russia."
~ Donald Trump Jr. Tweet, 10 December 2020

As the nation entered the Chanukah/Christmas season, it was clear the Grinch in Congress were celebrating having harmed millions of American families.

There were also at least two vaccines released to combat the Coronavirus. Assuming no virus mutation emerges to neutralize the inoculations, the full effect will felt in 2022. But the economy should be able to get back on track – China did it in twelve months.

Where America should be focused on its own problems, we saw Swamp Denizens voting to send its resources abroad to grow the nations that will be our enemies or economic competitors.

Pfizer has presented a 96% effective vaccine, China claims a 86% effective one which they will use as a tool to exert "soft power" on its Asian neighbors and those African nations where it wants to establish a commercial foothold. And the Russians are doing their own thing.

On 8 December, China"s state-run news agency Xinhua, ran an editorial that stated: *"China will not turn COVID-19 vaccines into any kind of geopolitical weapon or diplomatic tool, and it opposes any politicization of vaccine development."*

The editorial then asserted a 'cooperative good guy' position by saying: *"China's achievement in anti-epidemic response is not due to magic, but is based on a spirit that respects science and facts and places life and the people in the highest position, something that is reflected in China's unremitting efforts to promote global cooperation in COVID-19 vaccine development."*

At this point, people had forgotten Covid-19 was of Chinese origin and that, for the first month or two, China had hidden the emerging problem from the World Health Organization – and both WHO and China downplayed the potential for the global spread that is the current pandemic.

China's Covid-19 policies echo their general policies and the

New Silk Road agenda intended to spread the Chinese influence and world domination that was mentioned early in this book series.

The Chinese Communist Party is highly skilled in the arts of misdirection and camouflaging its activities. And this has become our 'Elephant in the Room'.

By the end of the Trump Administration, everyone should be aware of the role played by Biden boasting of his Ukraine *quid pro quo* blackmail threat that resulted in the removal of the Prosecutor General investigating the Ukrainian energy firm Burisma. Trump requested information about a Ukraine investigation – informally invoking the 1998 Clinton Treaty that authorized such requests.

Democratic members of the House of Representatives rushed to Biden's defense and used Trump's act of adhering to the law as grounds for an impeachment decided upon after the 2016 election.

Apart from enabling the Swamp Denizens to attack the man who proved to be a serious threat to their existence, the process of attacking Trump through impeachment over something associated with a minor Western European nation distracted from Trump's efforts to renegotiate Trade Treaties that had proved detrimental to the changing American economy whose balance of trade surplus had proven dependant on agricultural production.

Early on it was clear that Trump sought to repatriate the key industries that once defined and would again define the ability of America to be self-sufficient in times of global disruption.

Curiously, the pandemic has emphasized the importance of national self-sufficiency to the forefront of events, and Congress did what it could to suppress that reality.

The suppressed reality?

Over 90-percent of America's basic medical supply needs are provided by or via, China. This means, in event of a medical crisis, China could exert control by simply cutting medical supply lines.

China could end access to cellphones, laptops, along with a whole range of hi-tech network tools that have become an integral part of the everyday lives of those under thirty and rural businesses in the service-maintenance sector.

In a 3 December The Wall Street Journal op-ed, National

Intelligence Director John Ratcliffe made it clear *"that the People's Republic of China poses the greatest threat to America today, and the greatest threat to democracy and freedom world-wide since World War II."*

Effectively echoing what readers of this series were told in 2017 was the basic threat Trump's China Policy was attempting to address, Ratcliffe went on to assert that: *"The intelligence is clear: Beijing intends to dominate the U.S. and the rest of the planet economically, militarily and technologically. ... I call its approach of economic espionage 'rob, replicate and replace.' China robs U.S. companies of their intellectual property, replicates the technology, and then replaces the U.S. firms in the global marketplace."*

There are numerous issues China-related that are screaming for a resolution, but the MSM has locked the source of the screams away in a soundproof room.

We can go back to when Joe Biden was Vice President – his son Hunter flew to China with him on Air Force Two, and while there conducted "private business" which resulted in Hunter moving well over a billion dollars to the United States.

In theory, Hunter's use of Air Force Two for private business was a Vice Presidential conflict of interest and possibly illegal. But that issue got buried and MSM continued its attacks on Trump.

Fast forward to the days before the 2020 election, when a record number of voters had already cast their mail-in or absentee ballots and a brief story about emails on Hunter's laptop that reveal he was splitting the profits from China, Ukraine, and, apparently, other family operations where profits were made by leveraging Joe Biden's political position and influence.

Once again, rather than investigate, MSM buried the story.

On 9 December, Hunter Biden revealed his tax records were being investigated for possible tax fraud – and the investigations began in 2018 with the Justice Department examining his overseas business dealings. In the current phase, the laptop documents and related communications detailing his business dealings in China and Ukraine are now evidence in the probe which includes James Biden, the President elect's brother.

Supposedly, only first learned of the two-year investigation a few days before he went public with a formal statement issued by the Federally funded Biden transition team:

"I learned yesterday for the first time that the U.S. Attorney's Office in Delaware advised my legal counsel, also yesterday, that they are investigating my tax affairs. ... I take this matter very seriously but I am confident that a professional and objective review of these matters will demonstrate that I handled my affairs legally and appropriately, including with the benefit of professional tax advisors."

After the announcement, Biden's transition team released the usual statement of support: *"President-elect Biden is deeply proud of his son, who has fought through difficult challenges, including the vicious personal attacks of recent months, only to emerge stronger."*

It has been noted in the media that the issuance of Hunter's "personal" statement, using taxpayer funds, apparently is illegal – it was also an illegal use of taxpayer funds when he went to China.

Among the possible charges is the possibility that there was a combination of tax evasion and money laundering relating to the burying of influence that is extensive enough to involve both the FBI and IRS. These *"raise criminal financial, counterintelligence and extortion concerns."*

Readers of this series will recall the time spent on Joe Biden boasting, at an international forum, of his using $1 billion US loan guarantee as leverage to get Prosecutor General Viktor Shokin fired. That is an explicit example of a *quid pro quo* of the type the House Managers alleged warranted the impeachment of Donald Trump – the major difference being DJT was operating under the terms of a Congressionally approved information sharing treaty, and seeking data on the crime Biden bragged about committing.

Rather than look at nefarious activities involving Ukraine or China, House managers promoted a "Russia, Russia, Russia" chorus in which the Trump family was depicted as doing exactly what the Biden family was known to have done.

As we know, to justify the *quid pro quo* allegations against Trump, the House members leading the impeachment drive stated

Biden would be Trump's opponent in 2020 – and they asserted this even before the potential candidates had announced. Thus we know that process was rigged and that it had been predetermined that Joe Biden would be the candidate of choice.

Again, as shown in the presidential chart on the rear cover of "2020 IMPEACH V HISTORY," Biden meets the traditional kinship requirement, but, while he is superior to Trump, he is inferior to the better candidate, Tulsi Gabbard. As we also know, the Democratic National Committee {DNC} exercised every opportunity to scuttle her candidacy.

So, it would appear that the election was "rigged" before the Democratic debates were scheduled. Does that mean the election or actual voting was rigged? Of course not.

But then came Covid-19 and there was an opportunity to acquire votes before the election and before any negative news could emerge. All that was needed was for the candidate – Joseph R Biden – to hide in his basement and not provide anything that could be used against him.

In November, Di Dongsheng, vice dean of the School of International Relations at Renmin University told his Chinese audience that Beijing had *people at the top of America's core inner circle.*

Di Dongsheng asked his audience, "*We know that the Trump administration is in a trade war with us, so why can't we fix the Trump administration? Why did China and the US used to be able to settle all kinds of issues between 1992 and 2016?*"

He answered: "*I'm going to throw out something maybe a little bit explosive here. It's just because we have people at the top. We have our old friends who are at the top of America's core inner circle of power and influence.*"

That answer told, or revealed to, everyone China had bought its way into the American business and political system. And then he removed all doubt about what had been happening since the days of Ronald Reagan and the Bush administration: "*For the past 30 years, 40 years, we have been utilizing the core power of the United States.*"

We know that, even though Trump had spawned a continued

and accelerated growth, he was attacked, and various polls showed Wall Street favored Biden.

Di Dongsheng illuminated his audience about the side China supported and why. He didn't need to remind his audience that, even though China was seen as a Communist nation, it's heart was and will always be that of a Capitalist Mercantile Society:

"During the US-China trade war, [Wall Street] tried to help, and I know that my friends on the US side told me that they tried to help, but they couldn't do much. But now we're seeing Biden was elected, the traditional elite, the political elite, the establishment, they're very close to Wall Street, so you see that, right?"

Di Dongsheng then spilled the beans on Hunter and exposed why he should be investigated: *"Trump has been saying that Biden's son has some sort of global foundation. Have you noticed that? Who helped [Hunter] build the foundations? Got it? There are a lot of deals inside all these."*

As John Ratcliffe told Tucker Carlson, *"There are a lot of people who, for economic reasons, don't want China to be our greatest threat. There are a lot of people who, for political reasons, don't want China to be our greatest threat in America, but the intelligence doesn't lie. China is our greatest threat and it's not even close. ... No other country has the capability of essentially taking away the American dream, and a specific plan to do so, and the intelligence is clear."*

How can China take away the American Dream?

If it can, what is its plan?

More important, does China wish to discard more than four millennia of historic tradition to become an expansionist power? Didn't it learn the error of that approach when the Mongol Temüjin Borjigin – the Great Genghis Khan – expanded their domain across Central Asia to the borders of Eastern Europe?

Europe is not to be conquered and subjugated, it exists to be a client region, a conglomeration of Silk Road customers who will happily provide their gold and silver for a few spices and silks.

Temüjin lived in the era between 1158 and 1227; in Europe, his era was preceded by the expansionist Scandinavia Viking era was a time of merchant seafarers who we chose to remember only warriors, but who effectively unified territory where Temüjin halted his westward journey. Historians usually date the Vikings between 793 and 1066, but they remained a cultural force until 1130.

The Viking era was also the period in which, during the Song Dynasty {960–1279}, China invented paper currency as a means of controlling trade and hard assets in the form of precious metals.

It is interesting the American Constitution limits states rights with regard to coin money or {Article I, Section 10} "... *make any Thing but gold and silver Coin a Tender in Payment of Debts.*" In this context, paper money and federally minted coins are deemed the equivalent of gold and silver – which is the system the Song Dynasty introduced across all the Chinese provinces.

With our focus on the POTUS Cousins and 4-Sisters, we have their ancestor Charlemagne {748-814} and his direct descendant whose daughters are our 4-Sisters in the 1170s – one or more of whom are the direct ancestors to all the American Presidents.

Those familiar with Biblical Prophecy, and Revelation eras, might realize these people all fall into the end of the first thousand years, which gives rise to the thousand-year period that culminates in the Apocalyptic war of 2033, which is itself the end of a pattern beginning with Hitler in 1931 – the timeline is explained in my 2014 book Biblical Prophecy: Are we in the Revelation Era.

China and America are both outsides of regions mentioned in or affected by, the Biblical prophecy. Their citizens have a choice to be part of cataclysmic events or to stand aside and be merchants to the world that emerges after the destruction.

Curiously, history explains an objective Trump recognized as he reshaped NAFTA into USMCA and initiated a "trade war" with China that was intended to repatriate the industries that "*economic espionage*" is said to have stolen replicated, and replaced.

But the fact is, Americans intentionally outsourced – forced upon China and other nations – its technologies.

"America" wanted cheaper prices, it didn't care if its lower classes were thrown out of work. All that mattered was the cost of consumer products was less expensive than the cost to manufacture domestically. Trump has striven to repatriate manufacturing and thereby ensure American independence from those regions which will be destroyed by World War Three.

Granted, he might not consciously understand that to be the reason underlying his actions, but, instinctively he understands the global economy is extremely fragile, and previous wars have shown just how easily supply lines can be disrupted.

While geographically, China (3,705,410 sq mi) is equivalent in size to the United States (3,794,100 sq mi), its population of over 1.393 billion people is more than four times that of the United States (326.7 million) and enables it to be a self-contained economy whose only weakness is a lack of domestic inventiveness. But the historic nature of Chinese society makes true inventive creativity difficult. Therefore the Chinese adapt to foreign inventions.

The American mentality that has taken over the Democratic Party, and characterizes the Republicans who associate or identify with "Lincoln Project" dishonesty, is the modern equivalent of the Shakespearian nobleman, Antonio, and Bassanio, both of whom had, in their way, squandered their wealth.

To their advantage, the Chinese work ethic is extraordinary.

In the early days of American railroad expansion, Chinese Coolies (unskilled laborers) had a work ethic that resulted in their being able to lay ten miles of track for every mile laid by their Irish counterparts – and to do it over mountainous or uneven terrain at a time when the Irish were dealing with level plains.

The historic culture of China reveres scholars – and grants the poorest scholar a position we might associate with the followers of Jesus who gave away their money and relied on the kindness of those to whom they preached for their support.

We can date Chinese scholarship to the year that marks the beginning of their calendar. In my 2012 book, 'Genesis of Genesis' you learned this was, within the Hebrew calendar system, *"fifty-two Metonic cycles from Enoch and seven years from the birth of Noah."* And you also learned that the Hebrew and Chinese systems are both based on the same 19-year Metonic cycle, with the Chinese system *"attributed to the reign of the Yellow Emperor, Huang Di, with an initial date of 2698BCE."*

But, our modern calendar is the Hebrew – something that occurred when a Scythian monk was tasked with the job of assuring a timeframe alignment between Passover and Easter; he achieved it by ignoring the actual date and history surrounding when Jesus was born and setting Year-One of the Christian calendar to the 198th Metonic node of the Hebrew system.

Now we have Di Dongsheng describing what China has been doing for decades. He assigns it to Reagan's era, but it began with Nixon traveling to China on 21 February 1972 and reinitiating the 1899 'open door policy' that encouraged free trade with China.

While John Ratcliffe described China's policy as one based on *"economic espionage 'rob, replicate and replace,'"* any historian specializing in Chinese history would tell you their actions are as old as the nation itself. Chinese mythology and modern yDNA testing have established that contact with the west dates to the era when the British megalithic calendar structures like Stonehenge were being built.

As was stated early in this series, Trump understands China to be a mercantile nation with a history of foreign trade operations that might well extend to the time of Moses and the formation of the Twin Tribes whose structure is echoed in the Chinese reliance on a melding of scholarship and trade that reveres those devoted to one or both. Western attitudes are geared more toward warriors and we see merchants attacked (Shylock or the one-percent) and scholars typified as *"absent-minded professors"* suffering from a syndrome that drops them into a fantasy world, a world that exists outside the mainstream of western culture, but are revered within the Hebrew and Chinese world.

We can look at levels of student debt in America or the way we characterize "white-collar" workers within the stereotype world where Jews and Asians are assumed to be the better class where the mothers push their children to move higher in the academic world.

There are no widely accepted "Li'l Abner" stereotypes among those who prize *"wisdom, knowledge, and understanding"* – rather, what we see Elizabeth Warren and others spouting targeted hatred of the "one-percent" who are different from those Di Dongsheng's   *"traditional elite, the political elite, the establishment, they're very close to Wall Street."*

Exactly who are the elite establishment types Di Dongsheng was referencing? Who are the individuals working against Trump's plan to repatriate industries and secure southern borders against illegal entry – and, far more important, against drug smuggling?

Once again we have a China connection.

We know there is a difference, because Harvard Law School Professor Warren isn't about to attack Harvard or its graduates, and Nancy Pelosi is not about to attack her husband Paul Francis Pelosi, who heads Financial Leasing Services, Inc, nor would she attack those in his elite circle of influence who are counted among her most ardent supporters and financial backers.

The real estate and finance operations of Paul Pelosi connect Nancy to Wall Street, the establishment, and enhance the status she holds, as Speaker of the House, among the political elite.

Could the apparent overlap explain why she was out ignoring the pandemic, inviting people to visit Chinatown, and promoting superspreader activities would have certainly affect California cases when New York's Bill De Blasio was working so diligently to create his city's record death toll?

In August 2019, the media reported on several china related drug issues. One was a "tainted drugs" report which was part of a repetitive series of stories dating back to before 2007 and reflecting a Chinese quality control issue that has yet to be corrected.

Another story was about a deadly synthetic opioid painkiller known as Fentanyl, which is 50 times stronger than heroin and had been flooding the United States via the southern border that Trump has been trying to "wall-off." The drug is manufactured in China, transported to Mexico, and then across the border that Pelosi and others want to keep open – effectively giving the Chinese smugglers free rein to addict and kill Americans.

Could it explain why Pelosi opposed Obama's Secure Fence Act and the steel slat improvements Trump has been making to it?

Joe Biden bragged he blackmailed the Ukrainian President, Hunter Biden's laptop emails tell of the monetary amount that was daddy's cut of each influence-peddling deal. Now Di Dongsheng has spilled the beans and declared this has been going on for about as long as Biden has been in the Senate.

At the same time, Di Dongsheng was telling his audience about the control and influence China had, the media was reporting on the work of a Chinese national, Christine Fang or Fang Fang, who had been functioning as a spy targeting up-and-coming Bay Area local politicians who had the potential to make it big on the national stage. Which is to say, she was working in Nancy Pelosi's backyard and using it as a platform to expand nationally.

American intelligence officials revealed that Fang had played a Mata Hari role posing as a university student who then capitalized on her charisma, and romantic or sexual relationships to engage in extensive networking and involvement in campaign fundraising. She even had romantic connections with at least two Midwestern mayors and targeted California Congressman Eric M. Swalwell, a member of the House Intelligence Committee who was also a candidate in the 2020 Democratic Party presidential primaries.

According to the FBI, Fang's modus operandi relied on the "long game" strategy of striking up a relationship and then seeing if the individual moved up the line. Presumably, they would then be passed off to another agent.

Fang abruptly left the United States in 2015 and thus did not play a part in Trump-era politics. However, on 9 December 2020, Fox News host Tucker Carlson pointed out that *"As of tonight, with all this information public, Eric Swalwell, who has used his office to promote Beijing's talking points almost word for word ... who admits to a close personal relationship with an actual Chinese spy, who helped him get elected to Congress ... that man continues to serve on the House Intelligence Committee, where he has unrestricted access to classified information."*

And, recognizing that there is no question China supports Biden and opposes Trump, Swalwell had no issue asserting: *"I've been a critic of the president. I've spoken out against him. I was on both committees that worked to impeach him."*

It would seem Fang's long gameplay has borne fruit.

If we turn back to 7 August, we find Director of the National Counterintelligence and Security Center William Evanina warning the nation that China, Iran, and Russia could well be planning to interfere with the election and that, *"It's much easier for them to forge ballots and send them in, it's much easier for them to cheat with universal mail-in ballots."*

Knowing that we saw a significant drive to encourage people to vote early by mail. That created a potential two-fold problem: 1. The ballots were easier to tamper with; 2. Once cast, the ballots could no longer be influenced by media revelations of corruption – such as Hunter Biden's laptop emails, or the Christine Fang story which broke after Swalwell had received 76% of the vote in his run for re-election.

Then we had Pelosi's position as expressed on 10 December: *"I don't have any concern about Mr. Swalwell."*

Of course, there is no reason for concern. On 20 January, Biden will be President. At that point, he will either take actions to favor China, or he will continue Trump's agenda of repatriating the various industries that are critical to national security and the health and well-being of America's citizens. Of interest will be his position of the Obama Fence or Trump's Wall – which he supported during the Obama-Biden administration and is necessary for the control of addictive drugs from Mexico or, as has been the case with Fentanyl, from China via Mexico.

Then too there is the issue of those pharmaceuticals that the nation needs and the recent history of contaminated drugs from China, taken in the context of the Wuhan Covid-19 virus, could infer a "conspiracy theory" that China has been targeting Americans who are defined as Baby-Boomers and constitute the older segment of European and American populations.

Consider this brief history of contaminated pharmaceuticals of Chinese origin.

- In 2007 and 2008, 81 people were killed by contaminated heparin, an anticoagulant (blood thinner) commonly used to prevent the formation of clots – an effect of Covid-19 seen in younger individuals.

- August 2018 – The Food and Drug Administration (FDA) broadened a recall of valsartan, a common blood pressure drug after batches were discovered to be contaminated with a potentially cancer-causing chemical.

- September 2018 – The FDA blocked all imports of drugs made with ingredients from a Chinese plant at the center of a massive recall of heart and blood pressure medications.

- January 2019, The FDA inspections of factories in China and India making carcinogen-tainted ingredients which forced dozens of recalls of blood pressure drugs.

- 13-month period from August 2018 to September 2019 saw FDA more than 50 recalls of blood pressure medications because the active ingredient valsartan contained jet-fuel contaminants estimated to cause cancer in one out of every 8,000 pill takers.

- October 2020, saw an Indian pharmaceutical company recall metformin tablets that contained higher-than-normal levels of a carcinogen – but the idea they include any carcinogen is a reality that needs to be addressed by Congress. But, as we have seen, unfortunately, Congress would rather rant about Trump's Tax Returns – a rant that infers the IRS audits were incompetently done.

The usual recipients of hypertension medications are heart patients and those over 60 who evidence high blood pressure as the plaque buildup causes stiffening and narrowing of the arteries – that narrowing is a common effect of high salt, pork, or saturated fat diets.

President Trump called on the US pharmaceutical industry to manufacture domestically and cease outsourcing to China. Since Nixon reinstated the "Open Door Policy" many active medication ingredients have been sourced from China. As a result, Americans are medically dependent upon Chinese goodwill and mercantile interests for the active ingredients that go into antibiotics, heart medicines, and other drugs older Americans need to stay alive.

That reliance is a threat to national security. And the squalid Chinese drug factory conditions pose a serious health risk for the nation – even US military personnel take medications from China. A war with China or one of its allies or puppet states could seriously weaken America's national defense.

The United States should NOT be dependent upon foreign

nations for basic needs like medications and medical supplies.

Nor should it be energy dependent – a fact that negates the abstract arguments about the causes and means to address Global Warming and emphasizes the importance of a diverse renewable energy grid. And that grid should not have centralized power sources such as nuclear power plants which are an easy target for hostile nations during times of global war.

As strange as it seems, America is dependent on China and India for its health and wellbeing. And, as we have seen with their response to Trump attempting to address that and other health issues, the Congress represented by Pelosi, Nadler, Schiff, Waters, Schumer, and the rest of the pro-impeachment crowd has made it clear that they believe concern for the wellbeing of Americans is an example of racist xenophobia.

A Third World War is another "Elephant in the Room." That there is a religion which holds it is due in this millennia, and there is a reasonable timeline that says it is likely to happen in 2033 – we need to look at the reality that the generation that is now taking power has no reason to care about that or Climate Change.

House Speaker Nancy Pelosi is 80-years-old; if she is alive in 2033 she'll be a 93-year old senile great-grandma who will be so out of touch with reality that she wouldn't notice a war. As is, she has shown she doesn't understand the concept that the pandemic closed her beautician's solon and that in a business location like that she was supposed to wear a mask – the mask she wears for show when standing twenty-feet from the media giving a speech to the press.

Granted, the idea Pelosi might develop dementia is unlikely – but possible. Women who develop dementia tend to have visceral fat deposits {belly fat} and are, on average, *71.6-years old at the time of their baseline assessment.*"

The medical community is revealing a great deal of data that affects the importance of our "elephants."

In Sweden, we saw a nation that faced the pandemic using masks and social distancing rather than lockdowns – and it worked.

The Swedes also discovered that food availability and eating habits, in men when they were entering puberty could have a very positive effect on their sons and grandsons. Normally that would mean little in a book like this. But we are now hearing about food shortages caused by the pandemic and lockdowns.

Perversely, based on the detailed Swedish studies, it would appear that the children and grandchildren of the 9-12-year-old boy, a faced with full season of hunger today, could gain an escape from heart problems and years of an extra healthy life.

Based on the study, 30-years could be added to their average lifespan – the pubescent boys on the Great Depression breadlines were the World War Two soldiers whose sons are now comfortably over the age of 75 and surprisingly healthy. Those who are hungry today might have children who live to 100.

CHAPTER TWELVE – Wrapping up
**"I am a liar. Born to lying, bred to it, trained to it by an
industry that lies for a living, practiced in it as a novelist."
~ David John Moore Cornwell
(19 October 1931 – 12 December 2020)
Commonly known as Novelist John le Carré**

Donald John Trump has been called a liar, John le Carré is another man who made a living out of creating myths people want to believe.

As I draft this conclusion, it is the eve of the Christmas that wasn't. A Christmas that vanished in the pandemic lockdown world of closed shops replaced by online shopping. The Roman gift-giving slave holiday shall be celebrated in a different fashion. All because a Chinese virus affected Western culture more than it did the Asian nation that gave birth to it – a virus that is culling the post-World War Two Baby-Boomer generation.

As I write this, the Pfizer vaccine is being distributed and it promises to do what it does and little more. In America, Long Island Jewish Medical Center in Queens, New York City, became the site of the first to receive the new vaccine, which was received by ICU nurse Sandra Lindsay; the second recipient was Dr. Yves Duroseau Head of Emergency Medicine at Lenox Hill Hospital, also in New York City.

In keeping with the times, we note that both recipients are African American Medical Professionals. Within two days, reports began coming in that indicate those with a history of allergies and allergic reactions were having a *"very rare"* reaction to the vaccine.

As a result, FDA officials indicated they were going to require Pfizer to increase its monitoring for anaphylaxis, and Pfizer quickly acknowledged that the vaccine is recommended to be administered in settings that have access to equipment to manage anaphylaxis – any adverse reaction should occur within a half-hour of vaccination, though it would usually occur within minutes or even seconds.

There were also reports of a virus mutation that might prove to develop an immunity to the vaccination and continue the culling.

Concurrent with this historic step in combating Covid-19, in Pennsylvania, the Electors convened to cast their votes for Vice President Joseph R. Biden as the 2020 President-elect.

As Biden assumes his place in the Oval Office, the economy will continue to struggle; the United States will continue the painful transition into the new era of American history – the second 56/7 quadrennial cycle.

Is there truth in the quadrennial periods echoing Stonehenge and some mystical rhythm of the universe? Or is it a coincidental falsehood – lie to accompany the newest age of liars?

Humans live on lies – Jesus was born on 25 December in our year 1, a year that happened to be the 198th Metonic Node of the Hebrew Calendar and current with the Roman Saturnalia holiday.

Jesus was born in our year one – which was four years after the death of Herod who, as the Bible tells us, died two years after Jesus and his family moved to Egypt.

Herod's death can be cross-referenced in the records of the Roman Empire and other contemporary sources – thus, it would seem, Jesus was born seven years old and after his birth, must have traveled back in time to allow Herod to threaten his life and justify the journey to Egypt.

It's an "Elephant in the Room" upon which was constructed a religion and culture. That culture then decided – in the name of a jew named Jesus, who they revere as a deity – to kill all Jews. It is where we get the Inquisitions and Nazi Holocaust. If one were to believe in resurrection, in a second coming of a Jewish "King of the World", then killing Jews would put an end to the return.

We chose the lies we believe. That choice then allows us to inflict harm on others while claiming to be serving the forces of "Good". It is one of the many ways Satan Votes as he drives events to their predicted conclusions.

Trump is a liar, and Captain Jack Sparrow (Johnny Depp) has said, *"You lied to me, by telling me the truth."* But then, as a culture, we prefer to take as truth that which is a lie. We need to see the Emperor's beautiful new clothes. And we can find no place *"Wisdom, Knowledge, or Understanding."*

We've alluded to the "Elephant in the Room", but its true

nature is, as everyone knows, though it occupies massive amounts of space and everyone must navigate around it, there never seems to be anyone who will acknowledge it exists. It is, in many ways, a manifestation of the mirror image of "The Emperor's New Clothes."

There is that which we chose to see, and that which we chose not to see, and both are manifestations of the false reality you have chosen to live in.

It doesn't matter that Trump lost. Fools will call him a loser.

But, as we know from experience, the magic of the 4-Sisters and POTUS Cousins prevails in any Western nation whose destiny is that survives and lead others into "the promised land" that will be a better world.

Fortunately, nobody believes any of that. We travel through time and space, evolving into whatever it is we will become before we become extinct.

For now, we have history and current events.

In 2016, an American Economic Review article by Alan S. Blinder and Mark W. Watson entitled *"Presidents and the US Economy"* stated a statistical reality: *"The US economy performs much better when a Democrat is president than when a Republican is."*

Bush-43 crashed the economy, Obama and demographics brought it back, and then Trump made it grow to record levels; now we have a Democrat, Joseph Robinette Biden Jr.

The question becomes, will be true to Democratic tradition? Or will he prove to be the "Manchurian Candidate," and sell-out the nation to China?

As we have seen with the Tea Party, throughout the Obama era, when the Birther Movement engaged in its effort to remove a lawful President, and then, beginning with the election results of 2016, with the Swamp Denizen revolt that yielded the impeachment in leu of the Birther nonsense.

It seems funny, that passing Birther silliness, the Obama was born into a family line whose branches were defined by one that had its roots in the founders and the 4-Sisters, and the other with roots in a British Colony turned free nation. One White European line and the other derived from Black African – a division included in the original Constitution as a means of apportioning the way the census should count what might be termed a class of involuntary immigrants to determine representation and the status of citizen.

When Obama took office, he showed that, in effect, America had come full circle. European and African could be one and also be President. Obama is also a tenth cousin of the first President, George Washington. Where Washington filled the first slot of the Stonehenge style 56-57, Obama filled those last two positions.

The Hebrew Calendar is based on the Stonehenge count of 56 stones marking 57 segments of an astrological or historic era. As we know, there were twelve tribes – but actually, thirteen when the Levites, the tribe without inheritance in the land, is included.

We have also mentioned that there was a twin tribe – their numbers were composed of the one that was composed of Scholars and the other composed of the merchants who supported them.

Now we are in an era when Progressives are pointing to the need to support Scholars – to use taxes on business to support all

The 56 signers of Declaration

Carolina - North:	William Hooper		New Hampshire:	Josiah Bartlett
	John Penn			William Whipple
	Joseph Hewes			Matthew Thornton
	George Clymer		New Jersey:	Abraham Clark
Carolina - South:	Edward Rutledge			John Hart
	Arthur Middleton			Francis Hopkinson
	Thomas Lynch, Jr.			Richard Stockton
	Thomas Heyward, Jr.			John Witherspoon
			New York:	Lewis Morris
				Philip Livingston
Connecticut:	Samuel Huntington			Francis Lewis
	Roger Sherman			William Floyd
	William Williams		Pennsylvania:	Benjamin Franklin
	Oliver Wolcott			Robert Morris
Delaware	George Read			John Morton
	Caesar Rodney			Benjamin Rush
	Thomas McKean			George Ross
Georgia:	Button Gwinnett			James Smith
	Lyman Hall			James Wilson
	George Walton			George Taylor
Maryland:	Charles Carroll		Rhode Island:	Stephen Hopkins
	Samuel Chase			William Ellery
	Thomas Stone		Virginia:	Richard Henry Lee
	William Paca			Francis Lightfoot Lee
Massachusetts:	John Adams			Carter Braxton
	Samuel Adams			Benjamin Harrison
	John Hancock			Thomas Jefferson
	Robert Treat Paine			George Wythe
	Elbridge Gerry			Thomas Nelson, Jr.

those who have amassed student loan debt in their pursuit of higher education.

The 13 original colonies included their own set of twins – the ones known as North and South Carolina. If we wish to hold to the analogy, we can note that, in 1795, North Carolina opened the first Public University in the new nation. However, the true role of a dual merchant-scholar colony or tribe belongs to Massachusetts – which is the home of Harvard, which had been founded almost as soon as the Pilgrims were settled in.

When we look at the Declaration of Independence, we see a document signed by 56 men who said they had enough of having to take orders from the British Royals. Though we tend to ignore the fact that those royals were also their cousins – which goes to explaining the Emoluments Clause of the Constitution. They had no interest in their President taking orders from his old world kin.

Fifty-six men, from thirteen colonies. signed the Declaration of Independence. Twelve colonies were quick to acknowledge the new nation, and one, Rhode Island, hesitated.

But that is history. Now we have an election and a President who yells fraud. There is fraud – the voting machines that changed votes are sufficient to show that. But there is no fraud in the fact that the superior POTUS Cousin and descendent of the 4-Sisters is the one who won – because the superior descendent always wins.

But that does not mean the nation shouldn't take the charges of widespread, outcome changing, fraud seriously. But, if we are to have honest elections in the future, we need to ensure any glitches or problems that have emerged from wide-spread early or mail-in voting are addressed before the Mid-Term Elections.

The pandemic has resulted in a superior involvement and a record-setting voter turnout. It was also an election where many were not voting "FOR Biden," they were, as dictated by four years of media propaganda, voting "AGAINST Trump."

As a salesman, Trump understands the realities that drove the election to the inevitable outcome. As a result, he understands that, over the course of the next two years, many will exhibit all the traits of "*Buyer Remorse*." And, if that can be harnessed now, in two years, and again in four, Trump's loyal followers will see the victories he is now promising them.

There are those who would like to see mail-in ballots become standard practice. But, if mail-in voting were to be adopted, the security and assurances, the transparency, that Trump is calling for, would need to be solidly in place. Both the 2020 election and any future ones relying on mail-in ballots, demand the nation adheres to the adage, *"Trust but verify."*

On 14 December, members of the Electoral College convened in their respective states and performed their constitutional duty – Joseph R Biden received 306 to Trump's 232; this should have bee the same as the Trump over Clinton victory in 2016, but because of seven faithless electors, Trump won 2016 by 304:227. It is the beauty of the Electoral College, even when the Electors say now to both leading contenders, the 4-Sisters descendant will win over the non-family member and, when two descendants compete, it is the POTUS Cousin (the more American) who will win.

That does not mean the right person wins. It only means that the winner will be the one the nation needs to have victorious.

In the case of Biden, we might be looking at someone who is a victim of "Absent-minded professor syndrome" – it is a condition where an exceptionally gifted individual appears to lack the ability to remember basic everyday things. This could result in routine data related gaffs or order of magnitude shifts of the type Biden evidenced throughout 2020.

In practice, the gaffes are related to the brain's data storage and retrieval process. This is a matter of brain capacity and the basic "wiring" that serves to link the storage-retrieval elements to the neural processing portion of the brain.

In Biden's case, we are aware that he had received surgery for dual brain aneurysms and that this type of operation removes brain tissue and severs established connections; as a result, his brain had to rewire itself – insert jumper connections – which then manifested in various ways. One noticeable element is that he now, routinely, adds a thousand {three zeros} to numbers he cites.

While we have heard of Trump's alleged dishonesty, Biden has openly bragged about his criminality. It's a point that demands the repeated mention. The Swamp Denizens are distracting people by referring to Trump or making sick jokes about how, after the inauguration, Trump will be going to prison.

Washed-up actress Debra Messing even made a homophobic joke about how, once there, Trump would become the inmate's "most popular boyfriend."

On 15 December, Messing slandered both the President and the nation, by alleging in a tweet: *"Trump has perpetrated violence on hundreds of millions of people. My hope is (and this is the first time in my life) that the tables are turned and he is the victim of perpetrators."*

Apparent, Messing is among those proudly boasting they can see the Emperor's New Clothes. The fact that the lawyers who served as House Impeachment Managers couldn't define a single statutory crime Trump has violated is beyond her comprehension when it comes to realizing that Trump has committed no crimes.

Yet, we know that Hunter Biden is on record has traded on the Biden name and influence – his emails even show she and other family members shared the wealth with Joe. There is even an email that identifies $400,000 in unreported income – the crime of tax evasion willfully committed by Hunter. And, if his father received any funds he failed to report then the President-elect is also guilty of tax evasion.

Dishonesty is a natural state for a politician. The question is, at this point in its history does the Nation needs a politician at the reins?

On 17 December, Trump made it a point to distance himself from investigations into the Bidens by tweeting: *"I have NOTHING to do with the potential prosecution of Hunter Biden, or the Biden family. It is just more Fake News. Actually, I find it very sad to watch!"*

Leading up to the end-of-year adjournment of Congress, the Politicians were playing games with the economic support needed to keep the nation's citizens and businesses afloat until the vaccine can be fully distributed.

While there was an initial $908 billion bipartisan framework for assistance, it excluded the checks that had been part of the first legislation. In response, Senator. Bernie Sanders of Vermont and

Republican Sen. Josh Hawley of Missouri joined forces to push for the must-pass spending bills to include $1,200 checks or they would work see that none of the legislation comes to a vote. In response, lawmakers seemed to concede that they would allow $600 checks to be included in the package that must-pass by 18 December – or the government shuts down.

The additional sticking-points are provisions that provide a liability shield for employers and state funding to effectively bail out states that have proved to be fiscally incompetent. At stake is the survival of what many have said is the most powerful nation in the history of the world.

Removal of state bailouts would free-up about $160 billion in funds that would cover stimulus checks of $600 per person for those who received $1,200 checks under the first stimulus package.

Thanks to Pelosi's delays and her failure to have the House introduce a rational and necessary clean direct check package, over the ensuing months nearly eight million Americans fell into poverty and many – individuals and businesses – face eviction resulting from their inability to pay rent.

While some are calling for a cancellation of rents during the pandemic, their intent is not to help those who are hurting – rather the goal is to bankrupt landlords and is only an extension of the true motivation behind the attacks on a landlord named Trump.

With Biden as the lawful President-elect awaiting the formal acceptance by Congress in January, those who hate landlords will need to find another means of venting their historic bigotry. In so doing, they can continue their efforts to destroy America.

Since World War Two, history has established the United States economy performs better with a Democratic president; there is also the classic observation that Republicans get us into wars, and Democrats get us out of them.

However, history also reveals Republicans as Progressives and Democrats as devout proponents of slavery.

Modern, post-FDR, history saw the political identities seem flip, but Trump seems to have returned things to where they were before FDR – Democrats in California and other states are pushing for a low wage, non-voting, undocumented immigrants to fill census slots in the same was the two-thirds-of-a-person counting of slaves had grown representation for slave states.

On a 16 December podcast, the Representative Alexandria Ocasio-Cortez declared that both House Speaker Nancy Pelosi and Senate Minority Leader Chuck Schumer were no longer appropriate leaders for the Democratic Party – as evidenced by their approach to the second stimulus package negotiations.

AOC made it explicitly clear: "*We need new leadership in the Democratic Party.*" But at the same time, AOC acknowledged she was not the person for the job.

As she said: "*It's easy for someone to say: 'Oh, well, why don't you run? But the House is extraordinarily complex. And I'm not ready. It can't be me. I know that I couldn't do that job.*"

But, given that Pelosi and Schumer are devoted to screwing America, the real issue becomes the ability of Joe Biden to follow Trump's lead, return us to prosperity, and expand the movements toward peace between Israel and the Muslim world.

We might still hear "Russia, Russia, Russia" continue to be shouted – and that would continue to grow after the 15 December news that multiple Federal Agencies were hacked from a suspected Russian source.

However, Russians play a long-game – they are traditional Chess Masters – and the modern game board is Climate Change.

How is Biden going to address the issue? Under Trump, the nonsense of the Paris Climate Accord – a scam designed to export climate gases to third world nations or places like China, where the enormous population creates the statistical nonsense of low per capita pollution units. Factually, the Climate Accord was designed to achieve nothing beyond "good optics," and Greta Thunberg has repeatedly made the point.

When dealing with the realities of Climate Change, it should be noted that both Russia and Canada stand to gain while those who live within 15 degrees latitude of the equator will lose.

A NYTimes article published on 16 December points out that "*Russia's Jewish Autonomous Region*" (JAR} is emerging as the future center of Russian agricultural wealth and prosperity that is derived from being located on the Chinese border.

Despite its name, what had once been a dumping ground for Russian Jews is now the home of fewer than 1,500 Jews; yet it is still an autonomous oblast (district) and the only one, aside from Israel, identified as officially a Jewish jurisdictional territory.

The main JAR industry is agriculture; as we know from the Trade War, China needs agricultural products which, until recently, could not be filled by Russia. But with the acceleration of Global Warming and the related changes in climate, agriculture is moving north and lands that were of low productivity because of the extreme cold are now enjoying the promise of an average annual temperature of around 55 degrees – the ideal average temperature for human habits.

In 2021, the Tongjiang-Nizhneleninskoye railway bridge is due to open – at which time it is expected to handle the shipping of roughly 3 million tonnes of goods and transport about 1.5 million passengers per year.

As the climate warms, agricultural production will expand.

Spring thaw is now a month earlier than it was just twenty years ago, and that means agricultural production can expand and new types of crops can be grown. Eventually, that will eat into the American market – and an economy whose balance of trade surplus depends on agricultural production.

Climate refugees are a variation on the human capital that created the United States and then spawned its growth at the turn of the last century. The United States of America will need people from the Latin nations to the south.

But it will need to be an orderly and controlled process that will see them resettled in areas where their existing skills are best utilized. Ideally, many will continue their journey north to Canada and thus assist that nation in expanding its agricultural assets.

America does not need migrant workers, it needs citizens – individuals who, initially might work farms, but whose children will become our next generation of 21st-century professionals.

America will also need to end its balance of trade reliance on agriculture – industries outsourced over the past four decades will need to be repatriated and expanded in an environment driven by 100% renewable energy. That also means we will need to find new ways to store the generated energy – something that does not rely on foreign rare-earth minerals.

Biden has indicated he buys into "The Green New Deal," but he has an agenda that focuses on actions that are separate from economic realities and the needs of the nation.

For America to survive and prosper, renewable energy must replace all forms of fossil fuel or nuclear-based energy. The source of that energy should, where possible, be point-of-use when talking about routine day-to-day use in rural communities. But it should also include major sources of energy feeding a general grid.

As we know, as part of his border security wall, Trump has suggested the incorporation of solar on the steel slat wall/fence and the expansion of solar in the southern regions destined to become less inhabitable as the climate warms. Of course, Trump's idea was dismissed – and those supporting The Green New Deal (GND) had failed to defend and take full advantage of his off-hand suggestion.

Part of that failure comes from the fact that Trump suggested it during a June 2017 trip to Cedar Rapids, Iowa for a rally where he also discussed improving rural Internet connectivity as part of an infrastructure improvement strategy.

As Trump told the crowd, "*We're thinking of something that's unique, we're talking about the southern border, lots of sun, lots of heat. We're thinking about building the wall as a solar wall, so it creates energy and pays for itself. And this way, Mexico will have to pay much less money, and that's good, right? ...Solar wall, panels, beautiful. I mean actually think of it, the higher it goes the more valuable it is. Pretty good imagination, right? Good? My idea*"

The fact it was his idea – and there is a knee-jerk rejection of all "ideas Trump" – and that it makes solid economic and Green senses, was sufficient to have it rejected as soon as it was suggested.

Then there is the reality that the Green New Deal did not begin to emerge in the Democratic Party until November of 2018 – fully 18-months after Trump initiated their ideas and stated a basis for achieving their objectives. Naturally, there was no support from House Speaker Nancy Pelosi, so the Sunrise Movement organized a protest to try to alter her position.

In February 2019, Pelosi exhibited the same attitude toward the Green New Deal that she has toward Trump.

This was the first week in February, when AOC unveiled her "Green New Deal" package, which included several programs that, a year later, the nation would have profited from having – health care for all, which would have to address issues related to the pandemic, plus a goal of eliminating American carbon emissions – Pelosi dismissed it with the words: *"It will be one of several or maybe many suggestions that we receive. The green dream or whatever they call it, nobody knows what it is, but they're for it right?"*

The opposition drew sarcasm from Trump who, in February 2019, tweeted: *"I think it is very important for the Democrats to press forward with their Green New Deal. It would be great for the so-called 'Carbon Footprint' to permanently eliminate all Planes, Cars, Cows, Oil, Gas & the Military – even if no other country would do the same. Brilliant!"*

By September 2020, Pelosi had felt a shifting political breeze and declared the climate crisis *"is absolutely a priority"* – if Biden were to be elect, which he was. She also lied about her 2007 motivation in support of increasing fuel economy standards at a time when America was in combat amid the oil-producing regions of the world.

Speaking of that era, in 2020, Pelosi claimed, *"The climate crisis was my flagship issue. President Bush was president [and] together we passed the most significant energy bill in the history of our country – the equivalent of taking millions of cars off the road."*

Interpreting Biden's slogan, Pelosi also claimed: *"When Joe Biden says 'Build Back Better' that 'better' includes building back in a way that is resilient, that is green, that protects the planet."*

But, where is the evidence that Biden has a better plan than Trump's solar wall and utilization of something we will need for national security and to deal with the coming climate migration as a source of renewable energy? Are they not opposing construction along the southern border and promoting an open border that will flood the nation with individuals who will take a generation or more to adapt to American culture? That is, assuming they do not change the culture to echo that of the failed South American nations.

It is impossible to reduce greenhouse gases without going solar or wind. Nuclear is there, but it generation a thousand-year stockpile of radioactive poison which is far worse than any climate effect of a little added heat or rain.

The focus on the "carbon footprint" is pure stupidity, and it is clear that President Trump understands that. As he clearly said, *"no other country would do the same."*

The signers of the Paris Climate Accord are hypocrites and con-artists whose actions are not going to help the problem. At best, their goals will be achieved two decades AFTER they can have any effect. Moreover, if the nation does not prosper, if it is not geared to live within the realities of both the new century and new millennium, whatever is done only hurts those living now.

There is a reality, it is seen when the population and mean temperatures since 1890 are overlaid. Global Warming perfectly tracks population growth and the use of traditional 19th-century energy sources throughout that period.

In 1900, the industrialized world had the chance to turn to electric vehicles but opted for gasoline. Until the 1960s, coal, and wood were still major sources of heat – just as they had been in the previous century. Then there was the conversion to oil, and that was followed by the introduction of natural gas – which, as old pictures of oil fields reveal, was originally burnt as it emerged from the oil wells.

But, those who are interested in the survival of the United States – rather than just enhancing their personal wealth – will be the ones at the forefront of the Green Revolution. And they might well find members of the Trump family are already there awaiting their arrival.

The time will come when people realize the liars were those who accused President Donald John Trump of being a liar. If that happens, many will realize that Trump was, at heart, a Progressive Democrat with a rarely seen knowledge of economics and rational approaches to reality.

Biden has said he would have listened to the experts, and in his administration will listen to them. So let's look at exactly what an expert said, as we were reminded in a 15 December tweet from someone named Glenn Greenwald: *"In May – after Trump said there'd be a COVID vaccine by year's end – MSNBC put on its medical expert, @IrwinRedlenerMD, to assure viewers that it was *impossible* – not unlikely, but "impossible" – for there to be a safe and effective vaccine ready before 2021."*

The reference to an optimistic tweet by President Trump on 14 May, which said: *"Good numbers coming out of States that are opening. America is getting its life back! Vaccine work is looking VERY promising, before end of year. Likewise, other solutions!"*

MSNBC host Brian Williams put this to Redlener: *"The American people were promised, the promised was held out that we would have a vaccine by the end of this year. Is that possible in your view?"*

Redlener's expert reply: *"No Brian. You know it's another day of POTUS in wonderland here. It is preposterous to make that statement and also to mislead the American people about what's possible and what's not possible. We could have a vaccine in two months if we wanted to forego the absolutely critical phase of long human testing to make sure that the vaccine works, and most importantly that it's safe. It is impossible to get that done by the end of the year.*

Another expert, Dr. Paul Offit – a Professor at the Perelman School of Medicine at the University of Pennsylvania and the director of the Vaccine Education Center at Children's Hospital of Philadelphia – also went on record: *"I think it's possible you could see a vaccine in people's arms next year — by the middle or end of next year. But this is unprecedented, so it's hard to predict."*

Trump was correct and the experts were off by six-month to a year. As a result, we can only hope that Biden does not rely on "experts." Instead, we must pray he has the optimistic instinct that Trump has repeatedly demonstrated to be far more accurate.

On 22 May, Dr. Redlener had taken part in a discussion of the timeline presented by Trump officials on when a coronavirus vaccine may be available. At the time, he referenced the Swine Flu complication that emerged years after it was made available and challenged Dr. Fauci on the use of any unproven vaccine.

In a 14 June interview, Redlener challenged Fauci's view that oral polio vaccine might have a role in the fight against Covid-19, saying: *"Suggestions that oral polio vaccine may have a role in temporarily preventing Covid-19 are provocative, but not really supported by the kind of evidence that would make many of us optimistic. It's far too early to suggest that OPV is some kind of miraculous, low-cost preventive measure," added the professor of pediatrics."*

Fauci was, of course, taking a professional approach to any means of attacking any new disease – see if there already exists a treatment that can be re-tasked.

In the case of OPV, the logic was basic – a weakened version of a live virus triggers a general immune response to any foreign organism; the human immune system then has time to develop pathogen-specific antibodies to combat the novel coronavirus. In effect, even though it is not designed to combat the specific virus, the process allows the natural immune response to kick-in.

Dr. Redlener was, in effect, challenging the idea that there is a natural mechanism to fight disease and medical science could make use of it.

Ever the devout pessimist, on 7 May, speaking as director of the Columbia University National Center for Disaster Preparedness, Redlener took the position, *"If we want to get back to work, I don't understand how we're going to do that, actually, without being able to test regularly, reliably, point-of-care, and rapidly get the results back in a few minutes."*

Then, speaking of those who had been infected but recovered, Redlener said: *"…, we may have immunity that lasts two or three months, and then those antibodies won't work anymore, or the virus to which we developed the immunity will mutate and no longer be susceptible to being killed off by those particular antibodies."*

And while he was saying there might not be long-term immunity, he also demonstrated knowledge of economic reality and stated: *"There, we're talking about the microeconomy, where we're saying to people, 'We need to get back to work because you need to be back to work.' It's not because it's going to affect the stock market. It's because we understand you need to pay your rent and cover your expenses, and you live in the world where many, many millions of people in the United States and billions of people around the world have to have their regular income, and if they don't, the local economies collapse, stores close, people are really stuck with their living expenses, and so on."*

That reality is something Trump recognized from the very beginning of the pandemic, and it is a reality we must hope Biden understands. Moreover, the pandemic should have taught us that we are not prepared for a truly modern global plague.

Yes, the development of a vaccine was achieved in a record-setting fashion – and, if it proves successful, Trump-Pence gets the credit. But there is something more important that falls on Biden-Harris to address.

A University of Southern California study revealed that 37-percent of students in families making less than $25,000 per year lack Internet access. These students are disconnected from remote learning and prevented from developing 21st-century skills. In New York City, among low-income families, nearly 23-percent of high school students lack access to Internet-based classes.

Since this would be prevalent in her Congressional district, this is something we would expect AOC to be screaming about. And it takes on even greater importance when we consider the move to online medical care.

Regardless of whether or not AOC complains about the lack of universal internet access, President Biden should ensure he has a Cabinet Secretary assigned to bring about a form of broad-based connectivity.

Biden faces problems. But that goes with a transitional era in which the old generation is being culled, technology is changing, and the old bogeymen are being put to rest.

On 20 December, Senator Mitt Romney (R-Utah) warned the recent cyberattacks against U.S. agencies and companies had the potential to "cripple" the national electricity and water systems.

Appearing on NBC's "Meet the Press", Romney said: *"It is an extraordinary invasion of our cyberspace. They basically have the capacity to know what we're doing. They even got into the agency that's responsible for our nuclear capacities, for our research with regards to nuclear weaponry."*

Cyberwarfare is modern "Terminator" – no cyborg needed – centralized computerized resources are easy prey and reduce the need for "boots on the ground" attacks. As Romney said, *"This is an extraordinarily damaging invasion. And it went on for a long, long time."*

We can end the Trump Card series with the reality – the age of the powerful nation-state has come to an end. We are now in the age where the powerful will be those with the "Wisdom, Knowledge, and Understanding" to think their way to victory.